THE SPIRITUAL & PSYCHIC
DEVELOPMENT WORKBOOK

A COURSE COMPANION

HELEN LEATHERS & DIANE CAMPKIN

PUBLISHED BY SPREADING THE MAGIC

Copyright Helen Leathers & Diane Campkin 2009
Helen Leathers & Diane Campkin assert the moral right to be identified
as the authors of this work.

ISBN 978-0-9930513-0-2

First Published in 2009 by Spreading The Magic
www.spreadingthemagic.com

Cover Design by Titanium Design Ltd.
www.titaniumdesign.co.uk

All rights reserved. No part of this publication may be reproduced, stored in a retrieval system,
or transmitted, in any form or by any means, electronic, mechanical,
photocopying, recording or otherwise, without the prior
permission of the publishers.

Please note that while we are happy for handouts to be copied for use in your circle,
group or workshop, the copyright remains ours and full credits must remain on each copy.
Copies of these can be downloaded from the 'Readers' Resources' section
on www.thepsychicworkbook.com

If you have found this book, it is for you.
We will walk and talk you through the process of
discovering and developing your own natural abilities.

It is also for us, and for others just like us,
because we have searched for this book for years.
We just never knew that we would be the ones writing it!

CONTENTS

INTRODUCTION 7

BEFORE YOU START 11

LESSONS
- LESSON 1: AURAS & CHAKRAS 17
- LESSON 2: COLOURS 27
- LESSON 3: SPIRIT GUIDES 35
- LESSON 4: HEALING 45
- LESSON 5: PSYCHOMETRY 55
- LESSON 6: CRYSTALS 63
- LESSON 7: DOWSING 73
- LESSON 8: CARD READINGS 83
- LESSON 9: ESP / TELEPATHY 91
- LESSON 10: OTHER METHODS OF DIVINATION 101
- LESSON 11: NATIVE AMERICAN WISDOM & TOTEM ANIMALS 109
- LESSON 12: WORKING WITH SPIRIT 117

WHERE NEXT? 126

APPENDICES
- HANDOUT 1: INTRODUCTION 129
- HANDOUT 2: CHAKRAS DIAGRAM 131
- HANDOUT 3: BASIC CHAKRAS INFORMATION 132
- HANDOUT 4: BODY/CHAKRAS OUTLINE 134
- HANDOUT 5: BASIC COLOUR INFORMATION 135
- HANDOUT 6: PENDULUM COLOUR CHART A 137
- PENDULUM COLOUR CHART B 138
- HANDOUT 7: 'CONNECTING WITH YOUR SPIRIT GUIDE' EXERCISE 139
- HANDOUT 8: BASIC CRYSTAL INFORMATION 140
- HANDOUT 9: 3-CARD SPREAD 141
- HANDOUT 10: ZENER CARD SYMBOLS 142
- HANDOUT 11: ESP RESULTS RECORD PAGE 143
- HANDOUT 12: PSYCHIC SYMBOLS 144
- HANDOUT 13: ANIMAL SYMBOLISM 145
- HANDOUT 14: COMPASS POINT CARDS 147

GLOSSARY OF TERMS 148

CONTENTS
(CONTINUED)

RESOURCES 150

RECOMMENDED READS 151

ABOUT SPREADING THE MAGIC 152

OTHER PRODUCTS AND BOOKS BY THE AUTHORS 153

INTRODUCTION

ABOUT THIS BOOK
There are many books available that will give you information on the various aspects of psychic development and how to go about it. However, this one's a bit different. It's a step-by-step workbook with lessons that you can literally follow through to the letter. If you want to, you can go back to previous lessons and do them again and again.

We know from experience that there are many people who wish to develop their psychic abilities but don't have ready access to courses, workshops, development circles or personal teachers. Our aim in writing this book is to provide everything that you need to start your spiritual development journey. You can work through it on your own, however, we have essentially created it as a tool to be used in a group setting or development circle.

Based on the ideal of working once a week, this workbook gives you a three month course to follow. By which time you should be comfortable with meditation and working with energy, and beginning to develop skills such as divination and spirit communication. Your intuition should also be greatly enhanced.

Each week you will work through the detailed format. Everything is included for you, so you don't have to do too much preparation, or rely on someone coming up with fresh ideas each week. If you find that you don't like some of the words used, or you feel inspired to write something yourself, for example an opening prayer, then go for it, we won't be offended! The more you work, the more you will be inspired.

ABOUT HELEN LEATHERS
I have always felt that I was surrounded by spirituality but in a down to earth and integrated way. I've seen spirit from a young age and have actively pursued a spiritual path since about the age of 19. I started to read tarot in my mid to late teens, trained as a complementary therapist and Reiki Master in my twenties and have actively sought to develop spiritually and psychically through workshops and groups throughout that time. I'm very drawn to nature-based paths as well as the Eastern concepts of Buddhism and energy work. I've taught Reiki at all levels to many people and run spiritual and psychic development courses and workshops. I hate labels, but if pushed would say that I am 'an open-minded, eclectic, pagan-oriented, natural spiritualist'. That should just about cover everything!

ABOUT DIANE CAMPKIN
Like Helen, I also had many psychic experiences when I was younger, although I didn't understand many of them at the time. By my early 20's, changing personal circumstances and a series of synchronicities led me to my first psychic development and healing group, one that I still belong to to this day. Wonderful teachers, courses and workshops followed and I soon progressed to doing Angel Card Readings for others, trained as a Reiki Master and now run workshops and courses myself. I cannot put a label on my belief system, it's simply my own, derived from my experiences over the years.

WORKING TOGETHER
A series of synchronicities led to our paths eventually crossing in 2002, and we quickly progressed to working together in circle on a weekly basis. Supported by the other wonderful members of our group, we found that our work together was both powerful and profound. We are both natural teachers so when this project began to develop, it made sense for us to pool our knowledge in order to pass something on to others and help them to begin their journey of discovery. We both believe that this path can be for everyone, not just the chosen few. We want to make spiritual and psychic development accessible and down to earth whilst acknowledging it's awesome and exciting nature.

OUR ETHOS

By writing this book we do not wish to portray ourselves as the definitive experts. We are the first to admit that we still learn something new every day. Nor are we saying that our beliefs or opinions are the right and only way. They are simply ours and they may change in time, after all, who says you have to hold the same ideas forever? As with all books of this nature, some parts of it will resonate with you more strongly than others. However, even the parts that do not resonate as much will provide a base of knowledge that will help you to develop your own belief system. We firmly believe that this is one of the most important things that you can do on your spiritual path, whilst maintaining an open mind and allowing others their own personal beliefs without judgement. We don't believe that there is a right or wrong way, just lots of different ways.

Additionally, we do not demand that spirit communicate with us, nor do we worship the devil! We believe in a creative, divine force and are happy for everyone who shares this concept to call that force whatever they wish. Our motto is and always has been, 'In love and light, always'.

This isn't a book about our philosophy or belief system. There would always be something we disagreed on to some degree, making a joint venture of that nature remarkably difficult. Although there will be an element of our beliefs that come across, this book is a guide, a workbook to help you get started in finding your path. Our beliefs, whilst possibly of interest to some, are kind of irrelevant in this context.

PSYCHIC VS. SPIRITUAL DEVELOPMENT

It's important to understand that psychic and spiritual development are different concepts. Being psychic basically means that you can 'read' a person through their energy field. In our case, working on a spiritual basis, or mediumistically, means that you connect with Spirit, such as a Guide or loved one who has passed over, who help to pass on messages or do work on this plane of existence. Spiritual development also involves developing your own thoughts on the different levels of existence and all aspects of life and physical death, our reason for being and our interactions with others.

It is possible for a person to be 'psychic' but not to develop spiritually and sometimes this can lead to their work being ego-centred. However, when you develop spiritually, you connect with people on a deeper level, in a more empathic way. Your work is heart-centred. You will also find that you naturally develop psychically at the same time.

We believe that the best way to approach this type of work is from a spiritual direction whilst actively seeking to develop psychically at the same time. By doing this we bring harmony and balance into our lives as we integrate all aspects of our being and become whole again. As this happens we see the world, other people and our relationships on every level in a different light, it opens our eyes and our souls. It causes us to remember who we really are and why we are here. All in all, we believe that it makes the world a nicer place to be.

DEVELOPMENT CIRCLES

A group of people working together for psychic and spiritual development is referred to as a Development Circle. When a group of people work together with the same intentions they usually develop faster than if they worked on their own. In a circle all are equal, every person brings their own unique qualities, energy and experiences to the group and they all learn from each other. They all contribute to the energy of the group and the higher the level of energy, the higher the spiritual connection and the better and faster the development becomes. (It could be likened to connecting to the internet via broadband rather than 'dial-up'.) The group becomes a supportive family-like environment that is eventually much more than it starts out to be.

You should aim to have between 3 and 12 members in your development circle meeting weekly or fortnightly on the same day and time and, if possible, at the same venue. It is best to keep to the same people while you are undertaking this course, then only introduce people who you all feel comfortable with and whose energies gel with the groups. In our experience you shouldn't overly worry about this as those whose energies or intentions are not in harmony with the group don't stay long.

HOW THIS BOOK COULD CHANGE YOUR LIFE
Everyone comes to this type of work from a different background and for different reasons. Some people are never ready for this type of work in their current lifetime and that's fine. When Helen first started going along to workshops and courses she went mostly on her own. This was partly because few of her friends expressed an interest in attending, but also because it meant that there would be no one with her who would judge her.

Seeking out this type of development will change you, but it will be a positive change. You will become more sensitive, see the world differently, be more touched by the natural world and feel more at one with life. In a strange paradox, whilst feeling more a part of life, you may also feel more detached from your earthly experiences. There are reasons for this but for now, go with the flow, it is an enjoyable and fulfilling ride. Bear in mind that those around you who fear change may challenge you. This could be for a number of reasons, their own fear and doubts, or the fact that they care and worry about you. Your true friends will accept and support you without judgement.

You will also meet many wonderful people on this journey who will inspire, encourage and uplift you and who you will feel incredibly privileged to encounter. Some you will only meet in passing, others you may walk with on your path. However brief this time together may be, you'll always learn something as a result and should always count this time as a blessing. We have met some truly amazing people along the way. You don't have to travel to foreign lands or seek out gurus, they're all around just waiting for the right time for your paths to cross. Keep an open mind and an open heart and accept all that the universe is ready to give you, you'll be amazed at the seeming coincidences that will occur

We hope that your journey is as exciting, rewarding and fulfilling as ours have been.

In Love and Light Always,
Helen & Diane

BEFORE YOU START

SOME REALLY IMPORTANT STUFF

It is vital that you develop the harmony of the group of people who choose to work together.

It is also vital that everyone is comfortable with every activity that they undertake. No one must ever feel pressurised into taking part in an activity with the group. We would suggest that when you are starting out, if one person doesn't want to do something, you don't do it, no questions asked. If they feel uncomfortable with the whole lesson subject, they can simply choose not to attend that specific one.

We advise photocopying the 'Introduction' (Handout 1). This will go over what we will cover, our rules and guidelines for the group. Pass them on to your group members. You should then arrange an informal meeting a week or two before you start the course to discuss any questions or uncertainties that this may have raised. This is especially important for the person whose home or premises are being used.

Everyone should feel that they have a voice, and any problems or concerns should be discussed openly with all group members.

RULES

There are only three rules that we insist on in a circle:

1) Do not mix your spirits!

   In other words, no alcohol, or other mind-altering substances for that matter! Being under the influence whilst working in circle affects your ability and judgement. It also lowers your energy vibrations and your defences as well as your inhibitions. This can leave you and the rest of the group open to less positive energies or influences. This is non-negotiable as far as we're concerned.

2) Confidentiality

   Anything of a personal nature must not be spoken of outside of the group. This allows everyone to work with trust and develops a safe and supportive environment. This does not mean that spirit are going to divulge your innermost secrets to everyone, they don't work like that, but discussions can arise which can bring up sensitive issues and everyone needs to know that they can be open and honest with each other.

3) Stay Positive!

   This is extremely important. Positive energy is essential when working in a circle. Although working with spirit must be taken seriously, it can also be fun and indeed laughter can help to raise the energy vibrations. If you feel negative, depressed or simply under the weather, take a break and get an early night instead. You will be told how to bring yourself out of a meditation should you feel the need, and if you ever feel worried or uncomfortable in the group you must mention it. It would be wise to change the subject for a few minutes or to lighten the mood a little. Even taking a break, grounding and reaffirming your protection may be beneficial before proceeding. If necessary, close down, ground and finish the session. You can always repeat the lesson another time. Put some music on, have a laugh, make some tea and eat chocolate biscuits instead. No one should ever feel uncomfortable while working with Spirit and you should always feel confident enough within the group to voice your concerns and have them accepted by all. It is important as a group that you always adhere to this rule.

GUIDELINES

- Please be Prompt - If you know that you are going to be late let a group member know in advance so that they can wait for you.
- Keep it Regular - whilst it is understandable that things do crop up which can't be helped, it is preferable for group members to attend regularly to maintain group harmony.

- Food - it is not advisable to eat a large meal *just* before circle, equally a rumbling tummy during a meditation can be off-putting. Many people prefer to avoid eating meat before circle as they believe that it lowers their vibratory rate making it more difficult to work with the higher, faster spiritual energies.
- Health - if you're unwell it isn't advisable to work in circle as your energy levels will be low, but let the group know and they'll send you healing energy to help you feel better! If a person suffers from depression, anxiety or a similar mental health issue, especially if they are on medication for any of these conditions, we would strongly suggest that they avoid working with Spirit. They're more vulnerable to energy dips and should concentrate on getting well before developing in this way. However, learning about and taking part in healing groups would be beneficial.
- Personal Hygiene - a lot of books and teachings say that one should ritually prepare for spiritual work by bathing and dressing in particular clothing before starting work. This is not always possible, or necessary, however, cleanliness is always appreciated! Heavy perfumes can interfere with psychic work so should be avoided.
- Sharing - please do! Don't be worried about saying something silly, all contributions are welcome.
- Comparing - please don't! Everyone develops at different rates and finds certain things easier than others. Don't feel that you have to be the same as someone else or that you're not good enough, learn from and encourage each other.
- Working Space - it is ideal to use the same room each week. Before the meeting the room should be prepared. If possible, open the windows and air the room earlier in the day. Ensure that the room is warm and comfortable and that there is enough seating for everyone in the circle. You may want to burn some incense or place some fresh flowers in the room.

WHAT WE WILL COVER
Meditation; Auras & Chakras; Colour; Spirit Guides; Healing: hands-on & absent; Psychometry; Crystals; Dowsing; Tarot / Card Reading; ESP / Telepathy; Divination; Scrying; Totem Animals; Working or linking with Spirit / Mediumship.

TOOLS OF THE TRADE
You may want to collect a few things together for the group to use. To begin with you will only need a few basic things such as:
- Healing Book - A hard-backed notebook to write the names of those needing absent healing.
- Notepaper or individual notebooks for each person
- Pens / pencils
- Candles, a sturdy holder & matches
- Incense (ensure that all members are happy to use this as it can be quite irritating if someone has asthma or allergies)
- Tissues: it's quite common for emotions to be released when working through some of these exercises.

Other tools that you will need to use on this course will be listed in the Preparation Guide for each lesson. If you wish to be prepared well in advance, here's a list of what you'll need:
- One or more pendulum (brass, cut glass or a crystal / gemstone version)
- Pieces of different coloured card (any shape cut to around A5 size, strong colours are preferable)
- A4 sheets of white paper or card
- One or more bags of different coloured ribbons
- Coloured pencils (a mixture but including the main chakras colours, red, orange, yellow, green, blue, indigo and violet plus pink)
- Coloured chalks or crayons
- Large sheets of white paper and drawing paper – cheap flipchart pads are great.

- Dowsing rods
- A selection of crystals
- One or more sets of divination or tarot cards – group members may prefer to bring their own.
- A selection of different coloured pieces of fabric, shawls, scarves or pashminas.

To make life easier for you the meditations and visualisations in this book are available from the authors on audio CD to ensure maximum benefit to all participants. Please see page 154 for details.

The worksheets/handouts in the back of this book can also be downloaded for free from our website www.thepsychicworkbook.com, simply click on 'Readers' Resources'.

As you progress you will find that your collection grows, additionally group members will bring along their own things to certain meetings, such as tarot cards, crystals or reference books. In one of our groups we keep a sports bag that contains all sorts of things collected over the years (yes, these groups often last for many years).

In addition to these tools, each group member may like to keep their own journal. One of the best ways to do this is to use an A4 ring binder. Then you can section it off as you wish with dividers, and use it to keep the handouts that are included on this course. You can add interesting magazine and newspaper articles that you find and record your own meditations and discoveries. Also, if you forget to take your folder to a lesson or on a course, you can make notes and slot them in at a later date. You will soon build up an amazing reference guide for yourself as well as documenting your journey and development.

HOW TO USE THIS BOOK

Once you have a number of like-minded people who wish to work together to develop their psychic abilities and have arranged a convenient time and place to meet, you're ready to begin your course of study.

- Ensure that you have read the 'Introduction' and 'Before You Start' sections of this workbook.
- Photocopy the 'Introduction' Handout 1 and give a copy to each person in the group.
- Arrange and hold a pre-start meeting to discuss any issues that may have come up.
- Ensure that everyone has scheduled the meetings into their diaries to encourage commitment.
- Gather the basic tools together and you're ready to begin.
- A few days before each lesson, read through the Preparation Guide and ensure that you have all of the required tools. Remind any other members of the group who agreed to provide certain things at the end of the previous lesson. You will also need to photocopy the required number of handouts listed in the Preparation Guide.
- On the day of the meeting ensure that the room is prepared, there are enough seats for everyone and you have enough room for the work you are about to undertake. Open the windows, bring in some flowers or burn some incense to freshen the air. Gather together the tools that you require for the lesson you are working on and set out some water and glasses. It is important to keep hydrated when working.
- At each meeting simply work through the appropriate lesson as detailed in the next section of the book. All the words and meditations are written for you. The exercises are detailed for you and further study ideas are suggested. At the end of each lesson there's information about the following lesson so that everyone knows what's coming up and whether there's anything that they need to bring to the meeting. As each lesson covers a different subject there will be a varying amount of theory, practical and discussion each time. So, although the opening and closing sections will remain the same each time, there will always be something new to learn about, experience and do.
- It's inevitable that discussions will start during the lessons, and should be encouraged. They're important for your own understanding of the subject, your personal growth and for the bonding of the group. However, it's also important to keep on track and these discussions can always be continued afterwards over a cup of tea. We know how easy it is to carry on way into the night!
- This course of lessons can be repeated as often as you wish as you will always benefit from the information, exercises and meditations. You may feel confident enough to investigate other subjects

further yourselves, or alternatively, our 'Advanced Workbook' will allow you to continue your development within the same structure as this one.

Please note that while we are happy for handouts to be copied for use in your circle, group or workshop, the copyright remains ours and full credits must remain on each copy. Pdf downloads of the handouts may be made available to you by Spreading The Magic. No other part of this publication may be reproduced, stored in a retrieval system, or transmitted, in any form or by any means, electronic, mechanical, photocopying, recording or otherwise, without the prior permission of the publishers.

BASIC LESSON STRUCTURE

At the beginning of each lesson there will be a 'Preparation Guide' for the person organising it. Then each lesson will follow the same basic structure:

- Opening the Circle & Protection
- Healing
- Meditation / Guided Visualisation
- Lesson of the Week, Theory & Practical Work
- Closing the Circle & Grounding
- Further Study and what to bring for next time

In the next section of the workbook we provide a word-for-word format for each of the lessons that can simply be read out and followed. It would be nice if everyone eventually felt that they could take a turn at leading the group as this builds confidence and helps everyone to try something different.

It's essential when working that you ask your guides for protection, it's equally important that you 'ground' your energies at the end of a session. These elements are built into each lesson for you but you must be aware of them for when you begin working on your own. NEVER FORGET TO DO THESE TWO THINGS.

A NOTE ABOUT 'SPIRIT'

We try to use a capital 'S' to differentiate between 'Spirit', being the non-physical world beyond our own or the 'Higher Realms', and 'spirit' as the essence or soul of a person who has passed.

A NOTE ABOUT PROTECTION

When working spiritually we raise our energies and spirit beings are attracted to what we refer to as the 'light' that's generated as a result. Generally they are benevolent spirits who visit to offer their wisdom, messages of love and support or information to those they have left behind. However it's also possible to attract mischievous or even, in the worst-case scenario malevolent spirits. For this reason it is essential to put protection in place every time that you start to work on a spiritual or psychic level. We must add that we've never personally had a bad experience when working in Circle. We're sure that this is because we always ensure that we work correctly: putting protection in place before we begin, maintaining a positive atmosphere whilst we work and closing down and grounding our energies at the end of the session.

A NOTE ABOUT HEALING

We always include a time for Absent Healing within our workshops and circle evenings. We feel that in this way we are giving something back in return for the wisdom and knowledge that we receive from Spirit. When we wish well for others with pure intention our own energies are also enhanced as we connect with pure love energy and encourage oneness with Universal Energy.

It's a documented fact through various scientifically controlled experiments that people who are sent healing in the form of energy work or prayer feel better and recover quicker than those who are not, whether they know it's being sent or not. We know from personal experiences about the power of healing and in our groups we have had wonderful feedback from many people.

It's important however, to understand that healing and curing are not the same thing. For some it's their time to move on towards the spirit realms. Sending healing will help them to do so with peace and acceptance.

A NOTE ABOUT MEDITATION

Meditation in its simplest form is about bringing your focus into the present moment, rather than dwelling on the past, future or other concerns. It can be as simple as focusing on your breathing, on a candle flame or following a guided visualisation. Whichever method you employ, meditation is the single most powerful tool for your development. This workbook gives you an appropriate meditation for each lesson and encourages you to use all of your senses. If you find it hard to visualise or see with your mind's eye at first, don't give up simply try to engage your imagination and persevere. It will become easier in time. With practise you'll be amazed at how you can hone your skills. Don't be surprised if you pre-empt the guided visualisation by seeing something in your mind's eye before it's mentioned, you may even see something that isn't mentioned at all. These are all common occurrences and you will get used to them. Relax and enjoy the meditation experience.

HELP AND SUPPORT

It's a good idea to know how and where to find support and advice from like-minded people. Your local spiritualist church is often a good point of contact with some very experienced members. You may want to go along to some evenings of clairvoyance for some inspiration - you may even get a message of guidance for your endeavours! They may run courses and workshops and can prove to be very beneficial in pursuing your spiritual path and psychic abilities. But they're not for everyone, they are generally Christian based, so be aware of this if it's an issue for you.

It's also useful to have contacts should you have any questions or problems. If you come across anyone who you suspect may have a spiritual problem such as a haunting, point them in the direction of the Spiritualist Church. They 'get' the whole Spirit communication thing and will, hopefully, be understanding and sympathetic to their needs or problems. They usually run, or know of, a local Rescue Circle that can provide healing and advice or can put you in touch with an appropriate medium who is experienced in and can help with more serious concerns. When you first start out it can be exciting and tempting to try and help them yourselves, but it isn't something you should attempt without a lot of experience.

AND ANOTHER VERY IMPORTANT THING

During the course of this workbook we do talk about communication with Spirit, however, we appreciate that this may be a cause of concern for some people. Our golden rule is always to work with positive and highest intentions. Spirit should never hurt you or encourage you to do anything harmful to yourself or others or to act inappropriately. If at any time you're at all concerned by your experiences you should seek help from an experienced and reputable medium, healer, or if necessary a medical practitioner.

LESSON ONE
AURAS & CHAKRAS

PREPARATION
Well in advance of your meeting ensure that you have all of the tools that you require for this lesson. If not, find out if another group member has access to what you need.

Regular tools:
- Healing book
- Pens and pencils
- Paper
- Candles & matches if desired
- Box of tissues

Tools for this lesson:
- One or more pendulum
- Large sheets of white paper – a cheap flipchart pad is perfect
- Drawing pins or 'Blu Tac'
- Photocopy the required number of the following handouts:
    - 'Chakras Diagrams' Handout 2 - enough for 1 per person
    - 'Basic Chakra Information' Handout 3 - enough for 1 per person
    - 'Body / Chakras Outline' Handout 4 - enough for 1 or 2 per person

On the day of the meeting ensure that the room is prepared:
Are there enough seats for everyone and enough room for the work you are about to undertake? You should be seated, as much as possible, in a circle around the room, not too far from each other, so that you can link hands during the 'healing' work.
Open the windows or burn some incense to freshen the air.
Gather the required tools together. Call and remind anyone who has promised to bring something.
Set out some water and glasses.
Prepare some relaxing background music.

At the beginning of the meeting:
As people arrive ask them to add the names of anyone they know who needs some healing to the Healing Book. Remember that you don't need to put their full names and private information, first names, initials or nicknames will suffice. Whoever you intend to send the healing to, it will reach.

Once everyone has arrived and is comfortable then you can start.
As this is your first session, explain the following points to the group:
- The first section of the lesson will be a quiet meditative time during which you will be guided through a script (or following the audio CD if you have it).
- During the 'Healing' section you can all join in with asking for healing for individuals. The person leading the group will read through the healing meditation and then say, 'I would also like to ask for special healing for_____'. As with the Healing Book, you only need to mention first names, initials or nicknames. The healing will reach whomever it is intended for. When you've finished either say 'thank you', or gently squeeze the hand of the person on your left to indicate that it's their turn to

say the same. If anyone wishes to say nothing, or say their bit in their head, that's fine, again, you can simply pass to the next person with a gentle squeeze of the hand. Once everyone has finished, the person leading can continue with the lesson plan.
- The theory and practical work follow and you will finish with a 'closing & grounding' visualisation.

Now work your way through the script and exercises for this lesson as detailed on the following pages.

OPENING & PROTECTION
Read the following script out loud to the group. It's a time of meditation so keep your voice calm and relaxed, reading in a fairly slow and controlled manner. Instructions are in brackets and italics. (Alternatively use the audio CD.)

- Let us take a moment to close our eyes and calm our minds.
- Concentrate on your breathing, allowing the breath to become deeper and slower.
  (Pause to allow everyone to take a couple of breaths in and out)
- Let us all mentally ask our Spirit Guides and Angels to draw close and create a circle around our own.
- We let it be known that we are happy to work with Spirit and that we only work in love and light. We ask that anyone from the spirit world who wishes to contact us only does so in love and light and with the highest intentions.
- We ask for your protection, guidance and wisdom as we blend our world with yours. *(Pause)*
- Let us blend and harmonise our energies as we sit together in circle.
- Let us send out a note of harmony to the person on our left. Visualise this as a pale pink mist coming from your heart area and moving towards the heart of the person sitting on your left. *(Pause)*
- As you continue to do this, become aware of receiving the same loving energy from the right.
- As we send and receive this energy, be aware of any changes in the atmosphere within the circle. *(Pause)*
- Have a sense of oneness with the group. *(Pause)*
- Now bring your attention back to yourself and the centre of your being, the lower abdominal area.
- Focus on your breathing; become aware of the rise and fall of your abdomen. As you inhale it will gently rise and as you exhale it will fall. *(Pause to allow everyone to take a few breaths in and out)*
- Have a sense of warmth here and in your mind's eye allow a symbol or shape to form. Imagine that this symbol or shape is sitting at and represents your centre. It may be a simple glow of light, a flame or a flower.
- With each in-breath visualise your symbol becoming larger, stronger or more open whichever is appropriate.
- With each out-breath, imagine that you are exhaling any negativity left from your day, or worries that you may have. *(Pause to allow everyone to take a few breaths in and out)*
- Now take your awareness to the soles of your feet, feeling their contact with the floor. Visualise lines of energy extending out from your feet and down into the ground. In your mind's eye, see these lines of energy as roots extending deep into the earth.
- Earth energy also travels back up through these roots revitalising and nourishing you.
- See this energy entering through the soles of your feet and travelling up through your legs to the base of your spine.
- At the base of the spine imagine that the energy becomes a sphere of deep red mist or light, as you visualise it, it becomes more vibrant in colour. *(Pause)*
- From this point a beam of energy leaves the red sphere and travels up towards the sacral area, just below the belly button. Here it forms a sphere of vibrant orange mist or light. As you focus on it, it becomes stronger in colour. *(Pause)*
- Gradually a beam of energy leaves the orange sphere and travels up towards the solar plexus, where it forms a sphere of clear yellow. With each breath, this yellow becomes stronger and brighter. *(Pause)*

LESSON ONE – AURAS & CHAKRAS

- Once more a beam of energy leaves this sphere and continues its journey up to the heart area. Here a sphere of mist or light begins to form, which you may see as either green or pink. Focus on this area for a few breaths allowing the energy to grow stronger and clearer and to expand. *(Pause)*
- Gradually a beam of energy leaves the heart area and moves upwards to the throat. Here it forms a sphere of clear blue. Once more, as you focus on this area, allow the colour to expand and increase in strength. *(Pause)*
- Now, visualise a strand of energy leaving the throat area and linking with the third eye area, just between and slightly above the eyes. Here energy will begin to form as before. You may see this energy as either a rich indigo or violet, whichever you prefer. Concentrate on this energy and visualise it increasing in strength. *(Pause)*
- Again, a beam of light extends upwards from this area moving to the crown. As it does so, become aware of another beam of energy coming down from above to meet the first. As they meet at the crown a sphere of pure energy begins to form. You may see this energy as either violet or pure white light. This connects you with the higher realms of Spirit.
- As you hold this vision for a few breaths the light grows and strengthens. And as it does so, the beautiful pure light begins to overflow down and around you, surrounding you in its wonderful energy. It fills your aura, cleansing, balancing and strengthening it. You feel safe and comfortable. You feel relaxed and light. *(Longer pause before moving on to the Healing script below.)*

HEALING

- Slowly open your eyes and join hands with those sitting to either side of you. This increases the flow of healing energy.
- We know that our Guides, Angels and loved ones in Spirit have come forward and that they surround us with their healing energies. We ask them to help us as we send out our healing today. *(Pause)*
- Visualise a pool of brilliant white light forming and growing in the middle of our circle. *(Pause)*
- This is a pool of healing energy from which we can all draw when we need to. Know that this universal healing energy will find its way to all of those for whom we request healing.
- We ask for healing for each of us here, for our minds, bodies and spirit.

(If there are absent members: We ask for healing for the members of our group who cannot be with us today.)

- We ask for healing for all of those on our Absent Healing List. Take a moment to visualise them standing the healing pool.
- I would also like to ask for special healing for _____

(Mention anyone else that you feel healing is really important for today. Gently squeeze the hand of the person to your left to indicate that it's their turn. Let everyone have a turn at saying this part before continuing with the script.)

- We send our healing thoughts to Mother Earth and to the plant and animal kingdom.
- Thank you.
- Release your hands but keep your eyes closed so that you remain relaxed and peaceful as we go in to our meditation. *(Brief pause before moving on to the Meditation script.)*

MEDITATION

- Ensure that you're sitting comfortably with your hands on your knees, palms facing upwards.
- Close your eyes.
- Take a deep inhalation, and breathe out slowly. Continue to breathe slowly and deeply.
- During this meditation you will always be safe and protected, you will feel relaxed and comfortable. If, however, there is anything that does make you feel uneasy, or you wish to come back out of the meditation, you can do so at any time by counting backwards from 3 to 1 and taking a deep breath in and out. You can then bring your awareness back to the physical body, particularly your feet and open your eyes.
- For now though, continue to breathe slowly and deeply, your body feels relaxed and your mind is clear.

- As you breathe images may begin to form in your mind's eye. Don't try to manipulate or analyse them, simply observe them. If you do not automatically see these images, simply imagine or sense them.
- Ahead of you lies a staircase or series of ten steps. Move towards them. At the bottom you can see a doorway. We're going to slowly go down these steps towards the door feeling safe and confident at all times. So moving down the steps on my count:
- 10, 9, 8, with each step feeling lighter and lighter.
- 7, 6, 5, feeling calm and peaceful,
- 4, 3, relaxed and light
- 2 and 1, you find yourself standing in front of the door. Reaching out you open the door and as you do so, a wonderful, warm light shines through from the other side, bathing your whole being in its rays.
- As you stand in this light for a few moments, your physical body is warmed through and your energy body is nourished and energised. This gives you a sense of comfort and completeness and offers further protection on your journey. *(Pause for a short while)*
- Today's journey is going to be for the purpose of creating a sanctuary, your sanctuary. Here you can meditate, create, heal or simply be. It is a safe place for you to retreat to, in meditation, at any time. You can meet with your guides here and begin all your inner journeys from this safe place.
- The rays of light subside and you can now see through the doorway to the other side.
- As your eyes adjust to the change in light, colours begin to form shapes. Your sanctuary lies ahead of you and may take any form you wish.
- Step through the doorway now, closing the door behind you and begin to explore the sanctuary. It may be complete already or may come together as you watch. If you do not see anything forming as yet, create it in your imagination. Your sanctuary is a safe haven just for you. How would you like it to look? It provides comfort and warmth, places to sit, perhaps an open fire, and there will be access to the outside, perhaps a garden. This is your space and you may alter it if you wish. It may also change from one visit to the next depending on your needs at the time. Take time now to explore, enjoy the peace and tranquillity of this place, observe the décor, the soft furnishings, pictures, furniture etc. There may be a room for learning, a place to sleep, a place to eat, just like any home. Or it may be that your sanctuary is somewhere outside, in nature. Enjoy your time here knowing that you are safe and protected and I will return for you shortly. *(Pause for 5 minutes)*
- It will soon be time to leave your sanctuary. So now make your way towards the room that you first entered, where the doorway to the stairs is.
- In this room there will be a table or similar piece of furniture on which you may find a gift from your Spirit Guides. You will know which item it is as it will not have been there previously and will have a faint glow to it.
- Take this item in your hands and thank your Guides and loved ones in spirit for their gift. You are able to bring the essence of this gift with you as you return to the physical world.
- Open the door that leads to the stairwell. Step through closing the door behind you.
- Know that your sanctuary is your own space that you can return to at any time for relaxation, guidance and healing.
- And keeping that sense of calm and wellbeing, it is time to head back up the stairs. So moving back up the stairs on my count,
- 1, 2, 3, breathing slowly and deeply,
- 4, 5, 6, your body is starting to feel heavier
- 7, 8, bringing your awareness back to your physical body,
- 9 and 10, on that top step now and when you're ready, step off the top step.
- **Bringing your awareness completely back to your physical body and this room, your contact with the chair, your feet with the floor. Slowly begin to move your fingers and toes, and in your own time, opening your eyes, fully awake and aware and in the physical world.**

(Watch for them starting to wriggle fingers and toes and keep an eye on anyone who doesn't do this. If a member of the group appears not to want to come back to the room simply repeat the last paragraph, in bold, but raising your voice so that it said slightly louder and firmer. Repeat a third time if necessary moving over to the person and at the end just saying their name and asking that they come back now in to the room, placing your hand gently on their shoulder.)

Spend a few minutes sharing experiences of the meditation. Remember that it's okay if someone fell asleep, could see nothing or did their own thing. If you're keeping a personal journal, you may wish to take some time to record you experience. Don't forget to date the entry.

THEORY: AURAS AND CHAKRAS
The following 'theory' section should be read aloud to the group. You may want to get others to join in and take it in turns to read.

Energy
A fundamental principle of spiritual and psychic development is 'energy'. Life is all about energy. Everything is energy. All matter vibrates at different rates depending on what it is. Take, for example, water. Slow down the vibratory rate of its molecules, through cooling, and it becomes ice. Speed it up, by heating, and it becomes steam.

In order to develop our skills it's important to have a basic understanding of some of the theories of energy on an esoteric level. When we're talking about energy in this way we are talking about the 'vital life force' that animates all living things. It has many different names from many different cultures: Ki; prana; chi; mana; some will call it god; love; divine source; the list is virtually endless. There are many theories about they way in which energy flows through us on a subtle level, disciplines such as shiatsu and acupuncture work on the premise that we have a system of energy channels much like our physical network of veins and arteries carrying blood. This is a useful avenue to explore as you develop but for now two fundamental subjects to begin our energy journey with are auras and chakras.

Auras
In eastern and esoteric teachings it is said that we exist at many levels. These levels are like overlapping layers of ourselves, taking up the same space but each at a progressively higher vibratory rate. Our physical body has the slowest vibratory rate (imagine it as the ice), making us solid, present in the physical world and therefore visible to others. Overlying our physical body are the etheric, emotional or astral, mental and spiritual bodies. Because of their higher vibratory rates, these are not visible to most people, although some who are sensitive can pick them up through sensing, feeling or seeing the energy given off by them. These emanations are what is termed the aura and each energetic body has its own. Auras could be likened to the electro-magnetic field that emanates from an atomic structure.

Our auras surround us three-dimensionally, extending above and below our physical body. The etheric aura is the simplest to see. It's actually colourless, appearing more like a mist or a thickening of the air around the body, like an outline glow (imagine it as the water). The emotional or astral aura is next and is usually the one containing colour. Its colours change depending on our mood, activity, health and spiritual development. The final two are the mental and spiritual/causal auras which extend far beyond our physical body and connect us with the higher levels of energy and spirit realms. (These higher levels are like the steam, gradually becoming more diffuse as it progresses.)

It's possible with practise and experience to learn to tune into a person's aura and pick up information from it, either visually or simply by knowing or sensing. Information that we may pick up could be the colours in the aura, its strength, any weak spots, imbalances or damaged areas.

The aura can be weakened or inhibited by poor diet, lack of fresh air, lack of exercise, lack of rest, illness, stress, alcohol, drugs, tobacco, negative thoughts or habits or by not protecting ourselves sufficiently from external negative influences.

When we meet other people or go into places or situations our auras are the first part of us that pick up on information in the form of energy. This is then filtered down to our conscious mind for interpretation and action. It's said that when we take an instant dislike to a person or place it's because the energy of our auras are not compatible for some reason. We are sure that most of you have met someone who you feel really drawn to, or conversely that you don't like standing too close to for some inexplicable reason.

The exercises in this lesson will demonstrate how we can affect others and be affected by those around us. It will demonstrate the importance of strengthening and protecting our energy field through a healthy lifestyle, positive thoughts and good visualisation.

CHAKRAS

Pass out copies of the 'Chakras Diagram' handout to everyone.

Within our auras, creating a central vertical column following the line of our spine, sit the chakras. These are wheels of energy that extend out, like funnels, usually to the front and back of us. The chakras take in energy from the universe then transform and redistribute it throughout our energy system. Eastern philosophies teach that in order for us to be whole, healthy, creative, and to continue to develop spiritually our chakras must be working in harmony with each other, allowing a positive, steady flow of energy.

There are seven major chakras. Each contains all colour vibrations but is dominated by one. This colour relates to its primary role. When visualising or sensing the colours, it's important to use your intuition and 'feel' which colour works best for you. Some people prefer to use violet at the brow and white at the crown but others like to use indigo and violet respectively. It's entirely up to each individual and it may well differ from time to time as well as from person to person.

There are also many smaller chakras including those in the palms of our hands – used particularly when giving healing, and in the soles of the feet – useful to visualise when grounding our energies.

The chakras are always open but to varying degrees. They can sometimes be too open, or for others not open enough. In either case it can be indicative of an imbalance in certain parts of our lifestyle.

The 'Opening', 'Protection' and 'Closing & Grounding' exercises and visualisations that we do in this workbook involve working with the auras and chakras. So you can see that having an understanding of them is a key element in developing our skills.

PRACTICAL WORK

Read out each exercise, one at a time to the group so that you are all clear as to what you're doing, then allocate a time to complete the exercise.

EXERCISE 1: Feel the Energy

- Sit comfortably in a chair with your feet flat on the floor.
- Place your palms together and focus your attention on their contact with each other. You may become aware of heat building up.
- After a minute or so separate your hands very slightly. Maintain your focus on the same place between your palms. Very slowly move your hands slightly away from and then towards each other, as though pumping the air between the palms. You should become aware of a feeling of resistance here.
- Gradually take your hands further apart and each time they come back together, still with that pumping action, make the gap between your palms larger and larger. Feel as though there's a ball of energy between your palms. This energy has been created through the smaller chakras in the palms of your hands using your auric energy.
- You can play with the energy with practise. Move your hands around so that you can feel the edges of the ball.

- You will find, in time that this skill has other uses, but for now, it assists you in beginning to feel the auric energy that we talk of and activating the sense of feeling in your hands.

EXERCISE 2: Feel the Aura
Work in pairs for this exercise.
- One of you (the subject) should stand or sit in a chair.
- The other should slowly walk towards the subject with hands outstretched, if you feel that you wish to pause then do so. This is probably the edge of an auric layer, most likely the emotional aura. At this point, slowly move your hands around the outline of the subject at the same distance from their physical body. You may feel hot or cold spots, these can indicate energy blockages and can sometimes relate to physical problems as well. For example, heat around a joint or muscle area may be as a result of a sports injury or joint problem. This can take a lot of practise.
- Discuss any energy imbalance that you have picked up on with your partner and get their feedback too. Remember never to use this method in an attempt to diagnose physical ailments.
- Swap over and repeat.

EXERCISE 3: How you can Affect your Aura and Others
- Work in pairs for this exercise.
- One of you (the subject) should stand or sit in a chair.
- You must focus on your own energy field. Visualise it surrounding you and, when you feel that you're ready, visualise or feel it changing shape in some way. You can pull it in close to you, or push it out so that it gets bigger and bigger, or push it up high above your head. You could also visualise it as a specific colour, as very bright or even moving around you in a particular direction. Once you have chosen which one you are going to do, without telling your partner, focus on it completely until your partner notices the change.
- The second person can either sit opposite, walk around or simply stand next to the subject. It's their role to pick up on any changes or fluctuations in the subject's aura. You might feel it with your hands, as in the previous exercise, sense the changes or, if you're lucky, see them. Sometimes you will 'see' in your mind's eye and sometimes you will just 'know' what has changed, whichever way you find that you work best, go with it. Tell your partner when you pick up on the change and see if you are correct.
- The subject should try two or three different things before swapping over and repeating the exercise.

EXERCISE 4: How Others can Affect your Aura and You
- There are a number of ways that you can do this exercise. You can work in pairs or in larger groups.
- One person (the subject) should stand in the middle of the room and close their eyes. Be aware of any sensations that you feel around you. You may find that you sway or feel as though you are going to fall over in a particular direction. Keeping your eyes shut, tell your partner about the sensations that you are experiencing.
- The other person should stand in front, behind or to one side of the subject. From about two feet away you should use your hands to either push or pull the subject's aura in a specific direction. Work gently and slowly as the subject can be affected quite tangibly by this exercise.
- When the subject says or shows that they can feel the change, swap over and repeat the exercise.
- If you are working in groups larger than two, the others can observe the way that the subject is being affected. Alternatively, you could all stand around the subject at about four feet away, then one of you can move in slowly and quietly, standing nearer to them until the subject picks up on the energy change and says out loud where the person is or points to them. Take it in turns to be the subject and experience how others can affect your energy.

EXERCISE 5: Play the Hand Game
- Again working in pairs, stand or sit opposite each other.
- Place your hands in front of you so that your palms are facing those of your partner. One person (partner A) should close their eyes.
- The other (partner B) keeps their eyes open and move their hands slowly and deliberately around in the space between you. You should move one hand at a time, then pause to observe partner A. If they move their hands correctly, incorrectly or not at all, make a mental note and try again.
- Partner A should attempt to sense any movement and move their hands to match their partners – without physical contact.
- Partner B should make 10 changes then stop and give partner A feedback on how they did.
- Swap over and try it the other way around.
- You could try this with an observer and ask that the active partner simply move their hands into 10 places. The observer could record the number of 'hits' where the 'sensor' correctly moves their hands to mirror the others. As you get better, you should see an improvement on these scores.
- You may find that some people work better in certain couplings than others due to a closer relationship or a more instant connection.

EXERCISE 6: Take a Look
- Either work in pairs or as a group for this exercise.
- One of you (the subject) should stand or sit in a chair, preferably against a pale background. If this is not possible attach the large sheet of white paper to the wall behind using the pins or Blu tac.
- The other (or the rest of the group) should be sitting opposite, at least five feet away. Look past the subject at the air around or above them allowing your eyes to relax and go slightly out of focus.
- You may notice the air changing around the subject, perhaps appearing thicker. You may begin to see the etheric aura first, like a clear glow outlining the body. (If you remember the old 'ReadyBrek' adverts, the glow looks similar to that.)
- Eventually you may start to see colours or you may sense them in some way. Perhaps a colour, feeling or sensation pops into your head.
- Share what you pick up and if you are working in a group you may find that others are getting the same information as you.
- Swap over and repeat giving each person a chance to be the subject.

NOTE: Once you have trained yourself to see auras you may find that they just appear around people without you consciously trying to spot them. This is perfectly normal and further evidence of your growing psychic abilities. It can also allow you to see orbs and other visual phenomenon as your third eye chakra develops. When consciously attempting to view the aura of another person, please remember to be respectful and ask them if it's okay first. Remember that a lot of personal information can be seen or sensed in the aura. Plus, sensitive individuals will feel the intrusion if you stare at their aura without asking!

EXERCISE 7: Dowsing the Chakras
- Hand out the 'Body / Chakras Outline' handout.
- Working in threes, one person (the subject) lays with their back on the floor or a couch.
- The second person holds the pendulum in the subject's aura at the feet but in line with their spine. Allow the pendulum to hang free about 1-2 inches above their physical body. From here, slowly draw the pendulum along the mid-line of the body.
- You may feel the pendulum dragging through the auric energy at certain points and it may even appear to stop. If you feel that you want to pause, then pause. The key with this exercise is to use your intuition. At the chakras it will usually pause and either spin or make crossways movements.
- The third person can record the movements of the pendulum using the 'Body / Chakras Outline' handout.

LESSON ONE – AURAS & CHAKRAS

- If the pendulum spins it indicates that the chakra's energy is flowing well.
- However, if it spins widely, it can indicate that the chakra is too open. This may indicate that the person needs to be more protective of their energy as they may be losing energy to others or to the ether for some reason. The reasons will depend on which chakra is affected.
- If the pendulum spins but in a very small, tight, circle it can indicate that the chakra is too closed. Again the reasons depend on the chakra.
- If the pendulum does not move at all, this can also suggest that the chakra is not open enough.
- If the pendulum criss-crosses, let it continue to do so until it begins to spin. This can take some time and indicates that there is an energy blockage. The pendulum will work to free up the blockage and allow the energy to flow as it should. Reasons for this are similar to those when chakras are too closed.
- Refer to 'Basic Chakras Information to analyse your results.
- Swap around so that everyone gets the opportunity to try this exercise as the subject, dowser and observer.

CLOSING & GROUNDING
Once you have completed the exercises and had some discussion time, everyone should sit comfortably and complete the following meditation to close and ground their energy. Read aloud the following: (or use the audio CD.)

- Sit in a comfortable position and close your eyes.
- Bring your attention to your breathing and focus on this for a few breaths. *(Pause)*
- Take your awareness to the invisible energy field surrounding you and visualise it drawing in close around your physical body. *(Pause)*
- Take your awareness to the area just above your crown and see a sphere of light sitting here.
- Imagine that sphere of light shrinking in size until it's tiny, then sinking down through the crown of your head.
- See it slowly descending down past the brow. *(Pause)*
- Into the throat. *(Pause)*
- Then following the line of the spine, down, through your body, towards your heart area. (Pause)
- Down to your solar plexus. *(Pause)*
- Through the abdominal area. *(Pause)*
- To the base of your spine. *(Pause)*
- Now visualise the sphere of energy either leaving through the base of your spine, or dividing in two and sinking down through your legs and leaving through the soles of your feet.
- Feel this energy leaving you and connecting with the earth.
- Have a sense of downward movement, deep in to the earth. *(Pause)*
- Become more aware of your feet and your physical body.
- Let us take a moment to thank our Spirit Guides, Angels and loved ones in Spirit for their presence, protection and wisdom whilst we've been working. Knowing that they will always be on hand should we need to call on them. *(Pause)*
- **Now bring your awareness back to your physical body, the chair you are sitting on and your contact with the floor.**
- **Begin to bring some movement back in to your fingers and toes.**
- **In your own time opening your eyes, fully awake and aware and in the physical world.**

(Watch for them starting to wriggle fingers and toes and keep an eye on anyone who doesn't do this. If a member of the group appears not to want to come back to the room simply repeat the last three points, in bold, but raising your voice so that it said slightly louder and firmer. Repeat a third time if necessary moving over to the person and at the end just saying their name and asking that they come back into the room now, placing a hand gently on their shoulder.)

Check to ensure that everyone feels grounded before you finish the session. If not, get them to walk around for a little while. Stamping your feet or jumping up and down helps to bring you back to the physical world. If these don't do the trick, you can ground your energy very readily by eating a small amount of food such as a biscuit.

And another thing:
- Practise with the energy exercises in this book.
- Consider trying something like Tai Chi, Chi Kung or Yoga to help to connect with your energetic self.
- Find out more from books dedicated to auras and chakras and energy work such as:
    - 'How to See and Read the Aura' by Ted Andrews
    - 'Working With Your Chakras' by Ruth White
    - 'The Chakra Handbook' by Shalila Sharamon and Bodo J. Baginski
    - 'The Way of Energy' by Master Lam Kam Chuen

Next Time...
The next lesson will be covering the use of COLOUR in our spiritual and psychic work.
You will need to arrange for the following tools to be brought along:
- One or more pendulum
- A large sheet of plain white paper - a cheap flipchart pad is perfect.
- A selection of different coloured card – use strong colours such as the chakra colours, plus black. Cut the card into different simple shapes so that they will fit on a piece of A4 paper with space around all sides.
- Plenty of plain white A4 paper.
- Bag with a selection of different colours lengths of ribbon. (You may need more than one if you have a large group.)
- A range of coloured pencils, crayons or chalks – ensuring that you have the major chakras colours.

LESSON TWO
COLOURS

PREPARATION
Well in advance of your meeting ensure that you have all of the tools that you require for this lesson. If not, find out if another group member has access to what you need.

Regular tools:
- Healing book
- Pens and pencils
- Paper
- Candles & matches if desired
- Box of tissues

Tools for this lesson:
- One or more pendulum
- A large sheet of plain white paper - a cheap flipchart pad is perfect.
- A selection of different coloured card – use strong colours such as the chakra colours, plus black. Cut the card into different simple shapes so that they will fit on a piece of A4 paper with space around all sides.
- Plenty of plain white A4 paper.
- Bag with a selection of different colours lengths of ribbon. (You may need more than one if you have a large group.)
- A range of coloured pencils, crayons or chalks – ensuring that you have the major chakras colours.
- Photocopy the required number of the following handouts:
    - 'Body / Chakras Outline' – Handout 4 - enough for 2-3 per person.
    - 'Basic Colour Information' – Handout 5 - enough for one per person.
    - 'Pendulum Colour Chart' - Handout 6 A & B. Enough for one per person, you may wish to colour the sections in appropriately before the lesson starts.

On the day of the meeting ensure that the room is prepared:
Are there enough seats for everyone and enough room for the work you are about to undertake?
Open the windows or burn some incense to freshen the air.
Gather the required tools together. Call and remind anyone who has promised to bring something.
Set out some water and glasses.
Prepare some relaxing background music.

At the beginning of the meeting:
As people arrive ask them to add the names of anyone they know who needs some healing to the Healing Book. Remember that you don't need to put their full names and private information, first names, initials or nicknames will suffice. Whoever you intend to send the healing to, it will reach.

Once everyone has arrived and is comfortable then you can start.
Work your way through the script and exercises for this lesson as detailed on the following pages.

OPENING & PROTECTION
Read the following script out loud to the group. It's a time of meditation so keep your voice calm and relaxed, reading in a fairly slow and controlled manner. Instructions are in brackets and italics. (Alternatively use the audio CD.)

- Let us take a moment to close our eyes and calm our minds.
- Concentrate on your breathing, allowing the breath to become deeper and slower.
  (Pause to allow everyone to take a couple of breaths in and out)
- Let us all mentally ask our Spirit Guides and Angels to draw close and create a circle around our own.
- We let it be known that we are happy to work with Spirit and that we only work in love and light. We ask that anyone from the spirit world who wishes to contact us only does so in love and light and with the highest intentions.
- We ask for your protection, guidance and wisdom as we blend our world with yours. *(Pause)*
- Let us blend and harmonise our energies as we sit together in circle.
- Let us send out a note of harmony to the person on our left. Visualise this as a pale pink mist coming from your heart area and moving towards the heart of the person sitting on your left. *(Pause)*
- As you continue to do this, become aware of receiving the same loving energy from the right.
- As we send and receive this energy, be aware of any changes in the atmosphere within the circle. *(Pause)*
- Have a sense of oneness with the group. *(Pause)*
- Now bring your attention back to yourself and the centre of your being, the lower abdominal area.
- Focus on your breathing; become aware of the rise and fall of your abdomen. As you inhale it will gently rise and as you exhale it will fall. *(Pause to allow everyone to take a few breaths in and out)*
- Have a sense of warmth here and in your mind's eye allow a symbol or shape to form. Imagine that this symbol or shape is sitting at and represents your centre. It may be a simple glow of light, a flame or a flower.
- With each in-breath visualise your symbol becoming larger, stronger or more open whichever is appropriate.
- With each out-breath, imagine that you are exhaling any negativity left from your day, or worries that you may have. *(Pause to allow everyone to take a few breaths in and out)*
- Now take your awareness to the soles of your feet, feeling their contact with the floor. Visualise lines of energy extending out from your feet and down into the ground. In your mind's eye, see these lines of energy as roots extending deep into the earth.
- Earth energy also travels back up through these roots revitalising and nourishing you.
- See this energy entering through the soles of your feet and travelling up through your legs to the base of your spine.
- At the base of the spine imagine that the energy becomes a sphere of deep red mist or light, as you visualise it, it becomes more vibrant in colour. *(Pause)*
- From this point a beam of energy leaves the red sphere and travels up towards the sacral area, just below the belly button. Here it forms a sphere of vibrant orange mist or light. As you focus on it, it becomes stronger in colour. *(Pause)*
- Gradually a beam of energy leaves the orange sphere and travels up towards the solar plexus, where it forms a sphere of clear yellow. With each breath, this yellow becomes stronger and brighter. *(Pause)*
- Once more a beam of energy leaves this sphere and continues its journey up to the heart area. Here a sphere of mist or light begins to form, which you may see as either green or pink. Focus on this area for a few breaths allowing the energy to grow stronger and clearer and to expand. *(Pause)*
- Gradually a beam of energy leaves the heart area and moves upwards to the throat. Here it forms a sphere of clear blue. Once more, as you focus on this area, allow the colour to expand and increase in strength. *(Pause)*
- Now, visualise a strand of energy leaving the throat area and linking with the third eye area, just

between and slightly above the eyes. Here energy will begin to form as before. You may see this energy as either a rich indigo or violet, whichever you prefer. Concentrate on this energy and visualise it increasing in strength. *(Pause)*
- Again, a beam of light extends upwards from this area moving to the crown. As it does so, become aware of another beam of energy coming down from above to meet the first. As they meet at the crown a sphere of pure energy begins to form. You may see this energy as either violet or pure white light. This connects you with the higher realms of Spirit.
- As you hold this vision for a few breaths the light grows and strengthens. And as it does so, the beautiful pure light begins to overflow down and around you, surrounding you in its wonderful energy. It fills your aura, cleansing, balancing and strengthening it. You feel safe and comfortable. You feel relaxed and light. *(Longer pause before moving on to the Healing script below.)*

HEALING
- Slowly open your eyes and join hands with those sitting to either side of you. This increases the flow of healing energy.
- We know that our Guides, Angels and loved ones in Spirit have come forward and that they surround us with their healing energies. We ask them to help us as we send out our healing today. *(Pause)*
- Visualise a pool of brilliant white light forming and growing in the middle of our circle. *(Pause)*
- This is a pool of healing energy from which we can all draw when we need to. Know that this universal healing energy will find its way to all of those for whom we request healing.
- We ask for healing for each of us here, for our minds, bodies and spirit.

(If there are absent members: We ask for healing for the members of our group who cannot be with us today.)
- We ask for healing for all of those on our Absent Healing List. Take a moment to visualise them standing the healing pool.
- I would also like to ask for special healing for _____

(Mention anyone else that you feel healing is really important for today. Gently squeeze the hand of the person to your left to indicate that it's their turn. Let everyone have a turn at saying this part before continuing with the script.)
- We send our healing thoughts to Mother Earth and to the plant and animal kingdom. Thank you.
- Release your hands but keep your eyes closed so that you remain relaxed and peaceful as we go in to our meditation. *(Brief pause before moving on to the Meditation script.)*

MEDITATION
- Ensure that you're sitting comfortably with your hands on your knees, palms facing upwards.
- Close your eyes.
- Take a deep inhalation, and breathe out slowly. Continue to breathe slowly and deeply.
- During this meditation you will always be safe and protected, you will feel relaxed and comfortable. If, however, there is anything that does make you feel uneasy, or you wish to come back out of the meditation, you can do so at any time by counting backwards from 3 to 1 and taking a deep breath in and out. You can then bring your awareness back to the physical body, particularly your feet and open your eyes.
- For now though, continue to breathe slowly and deeply, your body feels relaxed and your mind is clear.
- As you breathe images may begin to form in your mind's eye. Don't try to manipulate or analyse them, simply observe them. If you do not automatically see these images, simply imagine or sense them.
- Ahead of you lies a staircase or series of ten steps. Move towards them. At the bottom you can see a doorway. We're going to slowly go down these steps towards the door feeling safe and confident at all times. So moving down the steps on my count:
- 10, 9, 8, with each step feeling lighter and lighter.
- 7, 6, 5, feeling calm and peaceful,

- 4, 3, relaxed and light
- 2 and 1, you find yourself standing in front of the door. Reaching out you open the door and as you do so, a wonderful, warm light shines through from the other side, bathing your whole being in its rays.
- As you stand in this light for a few moments, your physical body is warmed through and your energy body is nourished and energised. This gives you a sense of comfort and completeness and offers further protection on your journey. *(Pause for a short while)*
- Today's journey is going to help you to focus on your inner power and how to tap into it by connecting with the Universe.
- The rays of light subside and you can now see through the doorway to the other side. Your sanctuary lies ahead of you and you step through in to it's warmth, closing the door behind you. Make your way through your sanctuary to the exit that leads to your garden or outside space. Or your sanctuary may already be outside.
- You see a path ahead of you and you begin to follow it. Around you there are beautiful plants and trees, which seem to glow with an amazing energy. The air feels as though it's alive with a similar energy. You can feel it all around you, like a faint buzzing sensation.
- Ahead of you the path leads down three rocky steps to a wooded area. You reach these steps and slowly move down them, 1, 2, 3.
- Light is filtered through the branches and leaves of the trees and the woodland feels safe and protective. You feel happy to wonder through the trees, feeling the sunlight on your face and touching the bark of the ancient trunks.
- Soon you come across what looks to be the oldest, largest tree in the woods. You can feel the energy streaming from it and you cannot walk away from it. You lean your back against it's thick warm trunk with your feet firmly on the soil beneath. You can feel the tree's energy mingling with your own and as you stand against it. It seems as though you are truly becoming one with the tree.
- You feel your legs and feet extending further and further down into the earth as though they are the roots of the tree. And you can feel the power of the earth energy surging up through you nourishing your physical and energetic bodies.
- You can feel your upper body and arms extending upwards, reaching out along the tree's branches. Your arms and hands extend up into the sky. You can feel the warmth of the sun and the cool air brushing against you. You can feel heavenly energy streaming downwards enlivening your whole being. You feel strong and powerful. Enjoy this energy for a few moments. *(Pause for 2 to 3 minutes)*
- It is now time to return to your sanctuary, but know that this energy is always available to you simply by creating the awareness of your connection with the earth and with the heavens.
- Returning from the wooded area, you reach the rocky steps and move up them 1, 2, 3.
- Follow the path towards your sanctuary and go into it.
- Make your way to the doorway that leads to the stairwell. Open this door stepping through and closing it behind you.
- Keeping that sense of powerful creative energy surging through you, it is time to head back up the stairs.
- So moving back up the stairs on my count,
- 1, 2, 3, breathing slowly and deeply,
- 4, 5, 6, your body is starting to feel heavier
- 7, 8, bringing your awareness back to your physical body,
- 9 and 10, on that top step now and when you're ready, step off the top step.
- **Bringing your awareness completely back to your physical body and this room, your contact with the chair, your feet with the floor. Slowly begin to move your fingers and toes, and in your own time, opening your eyes, fully awake and aware and in the physical world.**

(Watch for them starting to wriggle fingers and toes and keep an eye on anyone who doesn't do this. If a member of the group appears not to want to come back to the room simply repeat the last paragraph, in bold,

but raising your voice so that it said slightly louder and firmer. Repeat a third time if necessary moving over to the person and at the end just saying their name and asking that they come back now in to the room, placing your hand gently on their shoulder.)

Spend a few minutes sharing experiences of the meditation. Remember that it's okay if someone fell asleep, could see nothing or did their own thing. If you're keeping a personal journal, you may wish to take some time to record you experience. Don't forget to date the entry.

THEORY: COLOURS
The following 'theory' section should be read aloud to the group. You may want to get others to join in and take it in turns to read.

Throughout history, many ancient civilisations have used colour and light in a variety of ways to treat disease, and to enhance wellbeing. These days colour is used in many ways, not only for physical healing, but to enhance moods and to rebalance energies. As discussed in the previous lesson, each of our main seven chakras has a corresponding, dominant colour. One use for colour is that should any of these chakras become unbalanced, the appropriate colour can help to restore harmony to your energetic systems.

Without realising it, we're already aware of how colour resonates in our everyday life. Think of the expressions that people use, such as 'green with envy', 'feeling blue' etc. In recent years organisations such as the NHS, the Prison and Police Services have recognised the impact of colour on our health and moods by painting hospital rooms, and holding cells in colours that promote healing or calm and Steiner schools use colour in the classrooms to assist children's natural development.

Another interesting aspect of colour is that many things can be ascertained about a person by the colours that they wear. Some people believe that individuals often subconsciously wear colours for a specific reason, for example someone who wears a lot of black will often want to fade into the background. By understanding more about colour, we can make informed choices about our clothing to help us with everyday situations, for example, blue is the colour of communication so is useful to wear when speaking in public.

Conversely, a dislike of a particular colour can be revealing. In Diane's case some time before embarking on her spiritual journey, she visited a personal colour analyst who advised her that purple would be one of her colours. She rejected this suggestion out of hand saying that she would never wear purple. Now, of course, the opposite is the case having embraced her spiritual side, purple is her favourite colour. She believes that her dislike of purple reflected the fact that she was not ready at that time to work with Spirit

It has been scientifically shown that light or the absence of it, can have an effect on the hypothalamus, pineal and pituitary glands and consequently on our health. Produced by the sun and filtered through our atmosphere, colour is the visible part of the electromagnetic spectrum (EMS) along with invisible radio waves, x-rays and microwaves. Visible waves sit in the middle of the EMS and are divided into seven different colours differentiated by their wavelengths.

We all know how other elements of the spectrum can have proven effects on our minds and bodies, for example the damage that is caused by over-exposure to u-v or x-ray radiation. Colour Therapy is based on the belief that the visible element of the spectrum, i.e. colour, can also affect the mind and body. Colour Therapy states that each part of the body, along with our emotions and mental states, respond to a specific colour. Treatment can take various forms:

- Sunlight focused on an area of the body
- Eating specifically coloured foods
- Drinking 'Rainbow Water' - water is poured into a coloured container and exposed to sunlight. The energy of the colour on the container is transferred to the water. The subject then drinks the water and absorbs the colour's energies.
- Colour breathing which requires you to visualise colours as you breathe deeply.
- Shining white light through coloured filters and directing it onto parts of the body.

- Wearing specific clothing colours. The physical and energetic bodies absorb vibration of the colours from these clothes.

Although colour therapists study in-depth courses over a long period of time, these are some simple ways that we can incorporate colour into our lives to enhance our health and wellbeing. The 'Basic Colour Information' handout will give you a starting point for working with and interpreting colour.

PRACTICAL WORK

Read out each exercise, one at a time to the group so that you are all clear as to what you are doing, then allocate a time to complete the exercise.

EXERCISE 1: Complementary Colours

This exercise gets you working with colours, thus making you more receptive to the rest of the exercises. On a colour wheel, the colour directly opposite another is called its complementary colour. These are:

red – turquoise

orange – blue

yellow – violet

green - magenta

- You will need pieces of different coloured card and larger sheets of plain white paper.
- Place one of the pieces of card on top of a piece of white paper.
- Stare at the card for about one minute, allowing your eyes to relax and go slightly out of focus.
- Quickly remove the piece of card so that you are now looking at the white paper.
- You will start to see the card's complementary colour on the white sheet.
- Practise this with all the different coloured pieces of card.

EXERCISE 2: Sensing Colours

You will need a bag of different coloured ribbons.

- Working in pairs, one person closes their eyes.
- The other passes them a ribbon from the bag and should keep notes for their partner.
- Keeping eyes closed, the person receiving the ribbon tries to sense what colour the ribbon is. Be aware of feelings such as 'heavy' or 'soft', 'light' or 'dark' etc. Some people may even be lucky enough to receive an image in their mind, e.g. a sun when holding a yellow coloured ribbon.
- Still with your eyes closed, tell your partner what you get so that they can make a record for you.
- You can try to guess the colour if you want to, although it's just as good to get a sense of how the colour 'feels'.
- Repeat the exercise several times, and then swap round so that you both have a turn at sensing.

EXERCISE 3: Dowsing for Colours

You will need the 'Pendulum Colour Charts'. We have provided two different charts, practise with both and find the one that works best for you. You will also need at least one pendulum.

- Holding the pendulum with one hand take a couple of breaths and ask that the pendulum moves to indicate 'YES'. It should slowly begin to move in a particular way, sideways, back & forth or in a clockwise or anticlockwise circle. Make a note of this then ask it to move to indicate 'NO', wait for the movement and make a note of it. Ask it to 'STOP' or say 'THANK YOU'.
- Now ask the pendulum to show you which colour(s) you are mainly vibrating in at the moment. Hold the pendulum over each colour in turn, and see how it moves.
- Now repeat the exercise asking which colour(s) you are most lacking in.
- You can also ask the pendulum to show you which colours you would most benefit from at the present time.
- Make notes of your findings and refer to the 'Basic Colour Information' to analyse them.

LESSON TWO – COLOURS

EXERCISE 4: Look for Colours
You may remember this exercise from last time.
- Either work in pairs or as a group for this exercise.
- One of you (the subject) should stand or sit in a chair, preferably against a pale background. If this is not possible attach the large sheet of white paper to the wall behind using the pins or blu tac.
- The other (or the rest of the group) should be sitting opposite, at least five feet away. Look past the subject at the air around or above them allowing your eyes to relax and go slightly out of focus.
- You may notice the air changing around the subject, perhaps appearing thicker. You may begin to see the etheric aura first, like a clear glow outlining the body. (If you remember the old 'ReadyBrek' adverts, the glow looks similar to that.)
- Eventually you may start to see colours or you may sense them in some way. Perhaps a colour, feeling or sensation pops into your head.
- Share what you pick up and if you are working in a group you may find that others are getting the same information as you. Refer to the 'Basic Colour Information' to analyse your findings.
- Swap over and repeat giving each person a chance to be the subject.

EXERCISE 5: Go Colour!
You will need a range of coloured pencils, chalks or crayons and plain paper. You may also wish to use the 'Body / Chakras Outline' handout as a starting point.
- Working in pairs, one should be the subject to begin with and simply sit and relax.
- The active partner should relax, close their eyes for a moment or two and then gently open them.
- Simply gaze at your partner. Remembering the work you have done on auras, can you see their aura at all? If so, draw a sketch of their aura. you can use the 'Body/chakras outline' to start if you like.
- If you can't see anything, don't worry. Allow yourself to intuitively sketch the colours you imagine to be around them.
- Try not to think too hard, simply pick up the coloured pencil that you are drawn to and begin sketching.
- Remember, there is no right or wrong, just your interpretation of the energy.
- When you're finished take a look at what everyone has done, refer to the 'Basic Colour Information' to analyse the colours. You may want to give your drawing or 'auragram' to your partner as a reading.

CLOSING & GROUNDING
Once you have completed the exercises and had some discussion time, everyone should sit comfortably and complete the following meditation to close and ground their energy. Read aloud the following: (or use the audio CD.)

- Sit in a comfortable position and close your eyes.
- Bring your attention to your breathing and focus on this for a few breaths. *(Pause)*
- Take your awareness to the invisible energy field surrounding you and visualise it drawing in close around your physical body. *(Pause)*
- Take your awareness to the area just above your crown and see a sphere of light sitting here.
- Imagine that sphere of light shrinking in size until it's tiny, then sinking down through the crown of your head.
- See it slowly descending down past the brow. *(Pause)*
- Into the throat. *(Pause)*
- Then following the line of the spine, down, through your body, towards your heart area. (Pause)
- Down to your solar plexus. *(Pause)*
- Through the abdominal area. *(Pause)*
- To the base of your spine. *(Pause)*
- Now visualise the sphere of energy either leaving through the base of your spine, or dividing in two

and sinking down through your legs and leaving through the soles of your feet.
- Feel this energy leaving you and connecting with the earth.
- Have a sense of downward movement, deep in to the earth. *(Pause)*
- Become more aware of your feet and your physical body.
- Let us take a moment to thank our Spirit Guides, Angels and loved ones in Spirit for their presence, protection and wisdom whilst we've been working. Knowing that they will always be on hand should we need to call on them. *(Pause)*
- **Now bring your awareness back to your physical body, the chair you are sitting on and your contact with the floor.**
- **Begin to bring some movement back in to your fingers and toes.**
- **In your own time opening your eyes, fully awake and aware and in the physical world.**

(Watch for them starting to wriggle fingers and toes and keep an eye on anyone who doesn't do this. If a member of the group appears not to want to come back to the room simply repeat the last three points, in bold, but raising your voice so that it said slightly louder and firmer. Repeat a third time if necessary moving over to the person and at the end just saying their name and asking that they come back into the room now, placing a hand gently on their shoulder.)

Check to ensure that everyone feels grounded before you finish the session. If not, get them to walk around for a little while. Stamping your feet or jumping up and down helps to bring you back to the physical world. If these don't do the trick, you can ground your energy very readily by eating a small amount of food such as a biscuit.

AND ANOTHER THING:

- Your work with the pendulum will have given you some insights into the colours that you most need to incorporate into your life. Here are some simple ideas to do just that:
    - Wear the colours that you lack or need – use the pendulum exercise to guide you.
    - Carry the relevant colour around with you in the form of a crystal
    - Eat foods of a specific colour
    - Where practically possible, surround yourself with a specific colour. Although you may not want to do anything as drastic as redecorating your bedroom, perhaps you could buy a new quilt cover or cheap bedspread so that you absorb the colour while you are sleeping.
- Look at colours that aren't attractive to you, and try to understand why.
- Why not focus on one colour for a whole day, or week at a time. Surround yourself in it, wear it, light coloured candles, eat food of that colour or carry crystals of that colour. See how it makes you feel or behave. Keep a diary of your findings and work through as many colours as you wish.
- Find out more from books dedicated to colour, for everything from decorating your home to aiding healing.

Next Time...
The next lesson will be covering the subject of SPIRIT GUIDES.
You will need to arrange for the following tools to be brought along:
- A pen and notebook.
- Drawing paper – a cheap flipchart pad is ideal.

LESSON THREE
SPIRIT GUIDES

PREPARATION
Well in advance of your meeting ensure that you have all of the tools that you require for this lesson. If not, find out if another group member has access to what you need.

Regular tools:
- Healing book
- Pens and pencils
- Paper
- Candles & matches if desired
- Box of tissues

Tools for this lesson:
- Drawing paper – a cheap flipchart pad is perfect
- Photocopy the required number of the following handouts:
    - 'Connecting With Your Spirit Guide' exercise – Handout 7 - enough for one per person

On the day of the meeting ensure that the room is prepared:
Are there enough seats for everyone and enough room for the work you are about to undertake?
Open the windows or burn some incense to freshen the air.
Gather the required tools together. Call and remind anyone who has promised to bring something.
Set out some water and glasses.
Prepare some relaxing background music.

At the beginning of the meeting:
As people arrive ask them to add the names of anyone they know who needs some healing to the Healing Book. Remember that you don't need to put their full names and private information, first names, initials or nicknames will suffice. Whoever you intend to send the healing to, it will reach.

Once everyone has arrived and is comfortable then you can start.
Work your way through the script and exercises for this lesson as detailed on the following pages.

OPENING & PROTECTION
Read the following script out loud to the group. It's a time of meditation so keep your voice calm and relaxed, reading in a fairly slow and controlled manner. Instructions are in brackets and italics. (Alternatively use the audio CD.)

- Let us take a moment to close our eyes and calm our minds.
- Concentrate on your breathing, allowing the breath to become deeper and slower.

(Pause to allow everyone to take a couple of breaths in and out)

- Let us all mentally ask our Spirit Guides and Angels to draw close and create a circle around our own.
- We let it be known that we are happy to work with Spirit and that we only work in love and light. We ask that anyone from the spirit world who wishes to contact us only does so in love and light and with the highest intentions.

- We ask for your protection, guidance and wisdom as we blend our world with yours. *(Pause)*
- Let us blend and harmonise our energies as we sit together in circle.
- Let us send out a note of harmony to the person on our left. Visualise this as a pale pink mist coming from your heart area and moving towards the heart of the person sitting on your left. *(Pause)*
- As you continue to do this, become aware of receiving the same loving energy from the right.
- As we send and receive this energy, be aware of any changes in the atmosphere within the circle. *(Pause)*
- Have a sense of oneness with the group. *(Pause)*
- Now bring your attention back to yourself and the centre of your being, the lower abdominal area.
- Focus on your breathing; become aware of the rise and fall of your abdomen. As you inhale it will gently rise and as you exhale it will fall. *(Pause to allow everyone to take a few breaths in and out)*
- Have a sense of warmth here and in your mind's eye allow a symbol or shape to form. Imagine that this symbol or shape is sitting at and represents your centre. It may be a simple glow of light, a flame or a flower.
- With each in-breath visualise your symbol becoming larger, stronger or more open whichever is appropriate.
- With each out-breath, imagine that you are exhaling any negativity left from your day, or worries that you may have. *(Pause to allow everyone to take a few breaths in and out)*
- Now take your awareness to the soles of your feet, feeling their contact with the floor. Visualise lines of energy extending out from your feet and down into the ground. In your mind's eye, see these lines of energy as roots extending deep into the earth.
- Earth energy also travels back up through these roots revitalising and nourishing you.
- See this energy entering through the soles of your feet and travelling up through your legs to the base of your spine.
- At the base of the spine imagine that the energy becomes a sphere of deep red mist or light, as you visualise it, it becomes more vibrant in colour. *(Pause)*
- From this point a beam of energy leaves the red sphere and travels up towards the sacral area, just below the belly button. Here it forms a sphere of vibrant orange mist or light. As you focus on it, it becomes stronger in colour. *(Pause)*
- Gradually a beam of energy leaves the orange sphere and travels up towards the solar plexus, where it forms a sphere of clear yellow. With each breath, this yellow becomes stronger and brighter. *(Pause)*
- Once more a beam of energy leaves this sphere and continues its journey up to the heart area. Here a sphere of mist or light begins to form, which you may see as either green or pink. Focus on this area for a few breaths allowing the energy to grow stronger and clearer and to expand. *(Pause)*
- Gradually a beam of energy leaves the heart area and moves upwards to the throat. Here it forms a sphere of clear blue. Once more, as you focus on this area, allow the colour to expand and increase in strength. *(Pause)*
- Now, visualise a strand of energy leaving the throat area and linking with the third eye area, just between and slightly above the eyes. Here energy will begin to form as before. You may see this energy as either a rich indigo or violet, whichever you prefer. Concentrate on this energy and visualise it increasing in strength. *(Pause)*
- Again, a beam of light extends upwards from this area moving to the crown. As it does so, become aware of another beam of energy coming down from above to meet the first. As they meet at the crown a sphere of pure energy begins to form. You may see this energy as either violet or pure white light. This connects you with the higher realms of Spirit.
- As you hold this vision for a few breaths the light grows and strengthens. And as it does so, the beautiful pure light begins to overflow down and around you, surrounding you in its wonderful energy. It fills your aura, cleansing, balancing and strengthening it. You feel safe and comfortable. You feel relaxed and light. *(Longer pause before moving on to the Healing script below.)*

HEALING

- Slowly open your eyes and join hands with those sitting to either side of you. This increases the flow of healing energy.
- We know that our Guides, Angels and loved ones in Spirit have come forward and that they surround us with their healing energies. We ask them to help us as we send out our healing today. *(Pause)*
- Visualise a pool of brilliant white light forming and growing in the middle of our circle. *(Pause)*
- This is a pool of healing energy from which we can all draw when we need to. Know that this universal healing energy will find its way to all of those for whom we request healing.
- We ask for healing for each of us here, for our minds, bodies and spirit.
(If there are absent members: We ask for healing for the members of our group who cannot be with us today.)
- We ask for healing for all of those on our Absent Healing List. Take a moment to visualise them standing the healing pool.
- I would also like to ask for special healing for _____
(Mention anyone else that you feel healing is really important for today. Gently squeeze the hand of the person to your left to indicate that it's their turn. Let everyone have a turn at saying this part before continuing with the script.)
- We send our healing thoughts to Mother Earth and to the plant and animal kingdom. Thank you.
- Release your hands but keep your eyes closed so that you remain relaxed and peaceful as we go in to our meditation. *(Brief pause before moving on to the Meditation script.)*

THEORY: SPIRIT GUIDES
The following 'theory' section should be read aloud to the group. You may want to get others to join in and take it in turns to read.

Spirit Guides act as messengers or advisors from the other side. They are like the spirit world's equivalent of our mediums. They help us when working spiritually and psychically, but also help to heal issues and restore balance in our lives. They can bring deceased loved ones closer to aid communication, help find and pursue our spiritual mission, show us past lives and future potential and act as advisors to groups working together regularly. Spirit Guides are advanced spiritual beings from higher planes who lend their energy and wisdom to help us to evolve spiritually.

There is much debate about how many Guides we have. We believe that everyone has many different Spirit Guides throughout their life. Some we may not even be aware of as yet but they still guide and protect us, perhaps speaking through our intuition and thereby sheltering us from physical harm. There are many people who believe that they have come out of an awful situation miraculously unscathed because 'someone' guided them to safety. That 'someone' is nowhere to be seen after the event. They can be people we have known who have passed on, or family members who we never or barely knew. Equally we may not have known them at all in this lifetime. Guides may be angels (or guardian angels) or may show themselves as children, animals or even mythical creatures.

Some people say that there are different Guides for different roles, such as:
- **Teacher Guide**: A Guide to assist in our studies, development and in the understanding of philosophy and universal laws.
- **Healer Guide**: These Guides may inspire us to look after ourselves better, eat healthier or get fitter. They provide healing energy and help to keep our energies aligned. They will also assist when we give healing of all forms to others.
- **Protector**: An extremely important Guide when we are actively working on spiritual and psychic development. Often one of the first to make themselves known to us, they protect our space and energies from negative influences and can provide strength, courage and energy when required. Usually large individuals with a strong, tangible presence, sometimes animals or mythological creatures.

- **Message Bearer**: These Guides amplify our intuitive messages, assist us in finding information and pass messages on to us if working mediumistically.
- **Helper Guide**: These Guides are often attracted to us in order to assist with a short term project or developing a particular skill.

Guides can come and go and be around for different periods in our lives. Even if they seem to have 'gone' they may have just taken a back-seat. The bond or attachment between us and them is always there.

Everyone seems to have an American Indian, nun or monk – why? Well these are people who have lived spiritual lives on the earth plane, therefore we can assume that they now exist on a high spiritual plane over there and are thus better placed to help us over here. However, Guides come in many forms and do not have to show themselves in this way. They could just as easily be a young person who appears to be no different to someone you might pass in the street. Guides only take on a form that we recognise because it is easier for us to visualise or understand.

Our Guides communicate with us in a number of ways. It might be a thought that magically appears in our minds or a gut feeling to take a particular turning or route. Mostly their communications are telepathic, which can make it feel tricky at first to communicate with them. With practise and trust you can talk to them. Learn to listen every time you get a thought or idea in your mind. Which ones seem insistent? Which ones come very quickly in response to a thought or question? Which ones do you tend to dismiss as 'probably just my own thoughts'? These are usually the ones from your guides. Often they speak to us in our dreams or through meditation. Some people believe that we are more likely to meet them when we sleep. At that time we remove our consciousness from the physical dimension into one of a higher frequency where we can re-connect with beings from other realms of existence. It is here that we work with our Spirit Guides and plan what we will do in the physical realms when we return to 'wakefulness'. We may or may not consciously recall these meetings. If they really want to make a point they will help to create a synchronicity in your life so that you will sit up and take notice. Synchronicities, in general, are experiences created by our soul to bring us into a greater awareness of what is occurring in our life. There's no such thing as a coincidence! If we meet someone 'by accident' it's because our soul and theirs has made a decision to meet, there are no accidents.

The best way to discover who your Guides are and how to communicate with them is through meditation. However, it does take time and practise. Trust your intuition. Some mediums may be able to tell you about your Guides, but we think that it's far better for you to try and make contact and then build a relationship with them yourself, even if this takes a bit longer.

Spirit Guides will not make our decisions for us. It is important to always remember that this is your life and you must live it. They will offer opinions and advice if you ask for it, but they will not tell you what to do, and it is always down to you to take responsibility for your own actions.

If you are scared of talking to Spirit, don't worry, this is a common reaction. Remember that we are always in control of any communication with Spirit. We exist on the physical plane and they are simply visiting us from the spirit realm. This means that *we* are the ones in control. Remember to always ask for protection and do your preparation before you start work, and ground when you finish. If you feel uncomfortable at any time, stop, and bring yourself back to the room. The role of a Spirit Guide is to offer loving, uncritical and unconditional guidance. Your Guides will *never* hurt you. Nor will they give you negative messages or encourage you to do anything harmful to yourself or others. If you hear any voices acting in this way then please seek help, as mentioned at the start of this workbook.

LESSON THREE – SPIRIT GUIDES

HELEN & DIANE'S TIPS:
* Firstly don't think you won't be able to do this, or that you don't have any Guides – everyone can and everyone does!
* Try not to have any preconceptions about who or what your Guide is.
* Remember that you are adjusting your brain to 'listening' for messages.
* At first you may only be able to keep the communication going for a very short time, with practise you will be able to work with your guide for longer periods.
* At first, using only Yes or No questions may be easier for you.
* Ask...pause...listen with your mind.
* If you have trouble 'hearing', try to visualise a screen with words and symbols appearing in answer to your questions.
* Ask questions about your Spirit Guide and their place in your life, e.g. What is their function? What is their connection to you? What can you do to find your mission? How many Guides do you have?
* Write down questions in advance and answers as you go along.
* Remember that it's normal for you to question whether it's a real communication or just your imagination. The only way to get round this is to keep trying and trusting that your Guide is there, until the point that your doubts disappear and you just *know*.

PRACTICAL WORK
Read out each exercise, one at a time to the group so that you are all clear as to what you are doing, then allocate a time to complete the exercise.

As mentioned in the theory, by far the best way of communicating with our Guides is through meditation, which is why the order of things is a little different for this lesson. Our meditation is designed for you to meet a Guide in your sanctuary and get a feel for who they are and what they look like. You may get more information, a name, way of calling them forward when you wish to communicate or information about their role and how they are going to help you. However, you may not get any of this. For some people it takes a few attempts at this meditation to contact their Guides but be patient and keep practising and you'll get there. The important thing is to know that they are around you at all times, you just haven't tuned into them as yet. If the meditation doesn't work for you, try the exercises that follow, and if it does, try them anyway to gain more information.

EXERCISE 1: Meditate
* Ensure that you're sitting comfortably with your hands on your knees, palms facing upwards.
* Close your eyes.
* Take a deep inhalation, and breathe out slowly. Continue to breathe slowly and deeply.
* During this meditation you will always be safe and protected, you will feel relaxed and comfortable. If, however, there is anything that does make you feel uneasy, or you wish to come back out of the meditation, you can do so at any time by counting backwards from 3 to 1 and taking a deep breath in and out. You can then bring your awareness back to the physical body, particularly your feet and open your eyes.
* For now though, continue to breathe slowly and deeply, your body feels relaxed and your mind is clear.
* As you breathe images may begin to form in your mind's eye. Don't try to manipulate or analyse them, simply observe them. If you do not automatically see these images, simply imagine or sense them.
* Ahead of you lies a staircase or series of ten steps. Move towards them. At the bottom you can see a doorway. We're going to slowly go down these steps towards the door feeling safe and confident at all times. So moving down the steps on my count:

- 10, 9, 8, with each step feeling lighter and lighter.
- 7, 6, 5, feeling calm and peaceful,
- 4, 3, relaxed and light
- 2 and 1, you find yourself standing in front of the door. Reaching out you open the door and as you do so, a wonderful, warm light shines through from the other side, bathing your whole being in its rays.
- As you stand in this light for a few moments, your physical body is warmed through and your energy body is nourished and energised. This gives you a sense of comfort and completeness and offers further protection on your journey. *(Pause for a short while)*
- Today's journey is going to be for the purpose of connecting with and meeting your most relevant Spirit Guide at this moment on your spiritual journey.
- The rays of light subside and you can now see through the doorway to the other side. Your sanctuary lies ahead of you and you step through into it's warmth, closing the door behind you. Or your sanctuary may be an outside space.
- Make your way to the exit that leads to your garden or outside space.
- Ahead of you is a gate. Walk towards the gate, feeling safe and comfortable. Open the gate and walk through.
- As you do so, you find yourself in a garden, the most beautiful garden you have ever seen. Flowers of every type and colour imaginable surround you. Their scent envelops you and you take a moment enjoying their extraordinary beauty. *(Pause)*
- You begin to walk through the garden now, entranced by the sights and scents, the colours and vibrancy of this magical place. Underfoot the grass is soft and springy and you feel more and more alive as you walk upon it, making your connection with Mother Earth.
- There are trees in the garden too, huge, ancient trees that seem so alive, their branches gently swaying in the warm summer breeze. They seem to beckon to you to walk towards them and sit against one of their sturdy trunks. Go towards the tree that you feel most drawn towards and sit down, resting against its trunk, surrounding yourself with its unique energy.
- As you sit by the tree you become aware of someone sitting down by your side. You may sense their energy, you may hear them, or you may even see them.
- You feel safe and happy in their presence.
- They may be familiar to you already, or they may be someone you don't recognise, but instantly you feel a connection between the two of you.
- Instinctively you realise that this other being is your Spirit Guide. Know that you are able to communicate with them and that you can ask them anything at all, that you can talk to them about anything and everything.
- I am going to leave you for a time to talk to your Spirit Guide, and I will return for you shortly. *(Pause for 5 minutes)*
- It will soon be time to leave your Guide. Before you leave, bid them farewell, but know that they will remain with you and work with you whenever you ask them to. Remember that you will take away with you all that you've learnt from your Spirit Guide, and that everything you've seen, felt or experienced will remain with you on some level, even if you don't recall all of it on your return.
- Begin walking back through the gardens that brought you to this special meeting place, again observing all the wonderful sights and sounds around you. The trees and flowers seem even more alive and vibrant now, and you feel re-energised and uplifted. As you walk through the gardens you remember all that you've talked about to your Guide. You feel safe and secure in the knowledge that they are always there for you, working with you for your higher good.
- Continue walking until you see the gate that led you into the garden. Pause for a moment to once again smell the wonderful aroma of the multitude of flowers. As you do so, you see on the gate a single flower, more exquisite than any you've ever seen before. This flower is a gift from your Spirit Guide,

LESSON THREE – SPIRIT GUIDES

a gift to remind you of the time you have spent together. If you wish, you can recall the image of this flower every time you want to connect to your Guide, and they will come straight to your side.
- Go through the gate now, and continue walking until you see the door that leads to your stairwell.
- Open the door that leads to the stairwell. Step through the doorway closing the door behind you. Know that this is your own space that you can return to at any time for relaxation, guidance and healing or to communicate with your Guides once more. And keeping that sense of calm and well-being, it is time to head back up the stairs.
- So moving back up the stairs on my count,
- 1, 2, 3, breathing slowly and deeply,
- 4, 5, 6, your body is starting to feel heavier
- 7, 8, bringing your awareness back to your physical body,
- 9 and 10, on that top step now and when you're ready, step off the top step.
- **Bringing your awareness completely back to your physical body and this room, your contact with the chair, your feet with the floor. Slowly begin to move your fingers and toes, and in your own time, opening your eyes, fully awake and aware and in the physical world.**

(Watch for them starting to wriggle fingers and toes and keep an eye on anyone who doesn't do this. If a member of the group appears not to want to come back to the room simply repeat the last paragraph, in bold, but raising your voice so that it said slightly louder and firmer. Repeat a third time if necessary moving over to the person and at the end just saying their name and asking that they come back now in to the room, placing your hand gently on their shoulder.)

Spend a few minutes sharing experiences of the meditation. Remember that it's okay if someone fell asleep, could see nothing or did their own thing. If you're keeping a personal journal, you may wish to take some time to record you experience. Don't forget to date the entry.

EXERCISE 2: Feel
- Calm your mind and relax your body.
- Take a few deep breaths.
- Ask your Guides to step forward.
- Ask your Guide for a physical sign so that you will know they are close.
- Make a mental note of any thing that you feel around you, a gentle touch, change in energy around you, heat, cold etc.

EXERCISE 3: Connect
- Keeping hold of your notebook or journal, continue to sit quietly.
- If you felt something physical during the last exercise, ask your Guide to repeat the sensation to prove the connection.
- Then still in relaxed state, draw your guide or write things down about him or her that you sense or see.

EXERCISE 4: Question
Work in pairs, one partner will be 'read' and makes notes (partner A), while the other does the reading (partner B).
- Using large sheets of paper, in case you feel the urge to start drawing, make a list of questions that you would like to ask your Spirit Guide. Examples are:
  Is my guide male or female?
  Are they tall or short?
  What are they wearing?
  What nationality are they?
  Do they have a recognisable 'job/status' (e.g. nun etc)?

What name or initial do they have?
What will they help me with?

- Sit opposite each other, partner A will have the sheet with questions, but partner B should also have a piece of paper and a pen or pencil.
- If you are partner B, close your eyes and attempt to link into the energy of your partner, and that of their Spirit Guides, to draw out more information about them. You may want to take hold of your partner's hand to help connect.
- Partner A should ask their questions out loud, one at a time making a note of the answers given by Partner B.
- The reader should answer with the first thing that comes to mind.
- Partner B should also sketch or write any further information that you get for your partner, and then give it to them as a gift.
- Always thank your Guides after you have worked with them.

CLOSING & GROUNDING
Once you have completed the exercises and had some discussion time, everyone should sit comfortably and complete the following meditation to close and ground their energy. Read aloud the following: (or use the audio CD.)

- Sit in a comfortable position and close your eyes.
- Bring your attention to your breathing and focus on this for a few breaths. *(Pause)*
- Take your awareness to the invisible energy field surrounding you and visualise it drawing in close around your physical body. *(Pause)*
- Take your awareness to the area just above your crown and see a sphere of light sitting here.
- Imagine that sphere of light shrinking in size until it's tiny, then sinking down through the crown of your head.
- See it slowly descending down past the brow. *(Pause)*
- Into the throat. *(Pause)*
- Then following the line of the spine, down, through your body, towards your heart area. (Pause)
- Down to your solar plexus. *(Pause)*
- Through the abdominal area. *(Pause)*
- To the base of your spine. *(Pause)*
- Now visualise the sphere of energy either leaving through the base of your spine, or dividing in two and sinking down through your legs and leaving through the soles of your feet.
- Feel this energy leaving you and connecting with the earth.
- Have a sense of downward movement, deep in to the earth. *(Pause)*
- Become more aware of your feet and your physical body.
- Let us take a moment to thank our Spirit Guides, Angels and loved ones in Spirit for their presence, protection and wisdom whilst we've been working. Knowing that they will always be on hand should we need to call on them. *(Pause)*
- **Now bring your awareness back to your physical body, the chair you are sitting on and your contact with the floor.**
- **Begin to bring some movement back in to your fingers and toes.**
- **In your own time opening your eyes, fully awake and aware and in the physical world.**

(Watch for them starting to wriggle fingers and toes and keep an eye on anyone who doesn't do this. If a member of the group appears not to want to come back to the room simply repeat the last three points, in bold, but raising your voice so that it said slightly louder and firmer. Repeat a third time if necessary moving over to the person and at the end just saying their name and asking that they come back into the room now, placing a hand gently on their shoulder.)

LESSON THREE – SPIRIT GUIDES

Check to ensure that everyone feels grounded before you finish the session. If not, get them to walk around for a little while. Stamping your feet or jumping up and down helps to bring you back to the physical world. If these don't do the trick, you can ground your energy very readily by eating a small amount of food such as a biscuit.

AND ANOTHER THING:
- Use the 'Connecting With Your Spirit Guide' Handout 7 to help you to communicate with your Spirit Guide on a regular basis, try it daily if you can.
- Now you have begun to build a relationship with your Guide, do some work with them! Ask your Guide to step forward when you are doing meditations and other spiritual and psychic work. Note how your Guide works with you. Are you working by hearing, sensing or seeing, or a combination? You may even start to sense them around you in everyday life. This should not be scary. It's nice to know that you are being watched over but if this at all unnerves you, simply ask them to leave you alone for a while.
- If you haven't yet connected with your Guide, keep at it. It can take weeks or months to really get to know who they are. However, always know that they are with you and they will be.

Next Time...
The next lesson will be covering HEALING.
You will need to arrange for the following tools to be brought along:
- Relaxing music
- Some cushions or hand towels and blankets to keep people warm during practical work
- If someone has a massage couch, this would be useful for the practical work
- A packet of wet hand wipes

LESSON FOUR
HEALING

PREPARATION
Well in advance of your meeting ensure that you have all of the tools that you require for this lesson. If not, find out if another group member has access to what you need.

Regular tools:
- Healing book
- Pens and pencils
- Paper
- Candles & matches if desired
- Box of tissues

Tools for this lesson:
- A massage couch if you own or are able to borrow one
- Cushions or a few hand towels to ensure comfort
- A couple of blankets
- Access to a hand basin or a pack of wet hand wipes
- Relaxing music

On the day of the meeting ensure that the room is prepared:
Are there enough seats for everyone and enough room for the work you are about to undertake?
Open the windows or burn some incense to freshen the air.
Gather the required tools together. Call and remind anyone who has promised to bring something.
Set out some water and glasses.
Prepare some relaxing background music.

At the beginning of the meeting:
As people arrive ask them to add the names of anyone they know who needs some healing to the Healing Book. Remember that you don't need to put their full names and private information, first names, initials or nicknames will suffice. Whoever you intend to send the healing to, it will reach.

Once everyone has arrived and is comfortable then you can start.
Work your way through the script and exercises for this lesson as detailed on the following pages.

OPENING & PROTECTION
Read the following script out loud to the group. It's a time of meditation so keep your voice calm and relaxed, reading in a fairly slow and controlled manner. Instructions are in brackets and italics. (Alternatively use the audio CD.)

- Let us take a moment to close our eyes and calm our minds.
- Concentrate on your breathing, allowing the breath to become deeper and slower.
 (Pause to allow everyone to take a couple of breaths in and out)
- Let us all mentally ask our Spirit Guides and Angels to draw close and create a circle around our own.
- We let it be known that we are happy to work with Spirit and that we only work in love and light. We

ask that anyone from the spirit world who wishes to contact us only does so in love and light and with the highest intentions.
- We ask for your protection, guidance and wisdom as we blend our world with yours. *(Pause)*
- Let us blend and harmonise our energies as we sit together in circle.
- Let us send out a note of harmony to the person on our left. Visualise this as a pale pink mist coming from your heart area and moving towards the heart of the person sitting on your left. *(Pause)*
- As you continue to do this, become aware of receiving the same loving energy from the right.
- As we send and receive this energy, be aware of any changes in the atmosphere within the circle. *(Pause)*
- Have a sense of oneness with the group. *(Pause)*
- Now bring your attention back to yourself and the centre of your being, the lower abdominal area.
- Focus on your breathing; become aware of the rise and fall of your abdomen. As you inhale it will gently rise and as you exhale it will fall. *(Pause to allow everyone to take a few breaths in and out)*
- Have a sense of warmth here and in your mind's eye allow a symbol or shape to form. Imagine that this symbol or shape is sitting at and represents your centre. It may be a simple glow of light, a flame or a flower.
- With each in-breath visualise your symbol becoming larger, stronger or more open whichever is appropriate.
- With each out-breath, imagine that you are exhaling any negativity left from your day, or worries that you may have. *(Pause to allow everyone to take a few breaths in and out)*
- Now take your awareness to the soles of your feet, feeling their contact with the floor. Visualise lines of energy extending out from your feet and down into the ground. In your mind's eye, see these lines of energy as roots extending deep into the earth.
- Earth energy also travels back up through these roots revitalising and nourishing you.
- See this energy entering through the soles of your feet and travelling up through your legs to the base of your spine.
- At the base of the spine imagine that the energy becomes a sphere of deep red mist or light, as you visualise it, it becomes more vibrant in colour. *(Pause)*
- From this point a beam of energy leaves the red sphere and travels up towards the sacral area, just below the belly button. Here it forms a sphere of vibrant orange mist or light. As you focus on it, it becomes stronger in colour. *(Pause)*
- Gradually a beam of energy leaves the orange sphere and travels up towards the solar plexus, where it forms a sphere of clear yellow. With each breath, this yellow becomes stronger and brighter. *(Pause)*
- Once more a beam of energy leaves this sphere and continues its journey up to the heart area. Here a sphere of mist or light begins to form, which you may see as either green or pink. Focus on this area for a few breaths allowing the energy to grow stronger and clearer and to expand. *(Pause)*
- Gradually a beam of energy leaves the heart area and moves upwards to the throat. Here it forms a sphere of clear blue. Once more, as you focus on this area, allow the colour to expand and increase in strength. *(Pause)*
- Now, visualise a strand of energy leaving the throat area and linking with the third eye area, just between and slightly above the eyes. Here energy will begin to form as before. You may see this energy as either a rich indigo or violet, whichever you prefer. Concentrate on this energy and visualise it increasing in strength. *(Pause)*
- Again, a beam of light extends upwards from this area moving to the crown. As it does so, become aware of another beam of energy coming down from above to meet the first. As they meet at the crown a sphere of pure energy begins to form. You may see this energy as either violet or pure white light. This connects you with the higher realms of Spirit.
- As you hold this vision for a few breaths the light grows and strengthens. And as it does so, the beautiful pure light begins to overflow down and around you, surrounding you in its wonderful energy. It fills your aura, cleansing, balancing and strengthening it. You feel safe and comfortable. You feel relaxed and light. *(Longer pause before moving on to the Healing script below.)*

HEALING
- Slowly open your eyes and join hands with those sitting to either side of you. This increases the flow of healing energy.
- We know that our Guides, Angels and loved ones in Spirit have come forward and that they surround us with their healing energies. We ask them to help us as we send out our healing today. *(Pause)*
- Visualise a pool of brilliant white light forming and growing in the middle of our circle. *(Pause)*
- This is a pool of healing energy from which we can all draw when we need to. Know that this universal healing energy will find its way to all of those for whom we request healing.
- We ask for healing for each of us here, for our minds, bodies and spirit.

(If there are absent members: We ask for healing for the members of our group who cannot be with us today.)
- We ask for healing for all of those on our Absent Healing List. Take a moment to visualise them standing the healing pool.
- I would also like to ask for special healing for _____

(Mention anyone else that you feel healing is really important for today. Gently squeeze the hand of the person to your left to indicate that it's their turn. Let everyone have a turn at saying this part before continuing with the script.)
- We send our healing thoughts to Mother Earth and to the plant and animal kingdom. Thank you.
- Release your hands but keep your eyes closed so that you remain relaxed and peaceful as we go in to our meditation. *(Brief pause before moving on to the Meditation script.)*

MEDITATION
- Ensure that you're sitting comfortably with your hands on your knees, palms facing upwards.
- Close your eyes.
- Take a deep inhalation, and breathe out slowly. Continue to breathe slowly and deeply.
- During this meditation you will always be safe and protected, you will feel relaxed and comfortable. If, however, there is anything that does make you feel uneasy, or you wish to come back out of the meditation, you can do so at any time by counting backwards from 3 to 1 and taking a deep breath in and out. You can then bring your awareness back to the physical body, particularly your feet and open your eyes.
- For now though, continue to breathe slowly and deeply, your body feels relaxed and your mind is clear.
- As you breathe images may begin to form in your mind's eye. Don't try to manipulate or analyse them, simply observe them. If you do not automatically see these images, simply imagine or sense them.
- Ahead of you lies a staircase or series of ten steps. Move towards them. At the bottom you can see a doorway. We're going to slowly go down these steps towards the door feeling safe and confident at all times. So moving down the steps on my count:
- 10, 9, 8, with each step feeling lighter and lighter.
- 7, 6, 5, feeling calm and peaceful,
- 4, 3, relaxed and light
- 2 and 1, you find yourself standing in front of the door. Reaching out you open the door and as you do so, a wonderful, warm light shines through from the other side, bathing your whole being in its rays.
- As you stand in this light for a few moments, your physical body is warmed through and your energy body is nourished and energised. This gives you a sense of comfort and completeness and offers further protection on your journey. *(Pause for a short while)*
- Today's journey is for you to receive healing energy from the higher realms.
- The rays of light subside and you can now see through the doorway to the other side.
- As your eyes adjust to the change in light, you can see your sanctuary ahead of you and you step through the doorway into the peace and tranquillity closing the door behind you.
- Find a comfortable place in your sanctuary to sit or lie down. Ask that you be given healing from the

Angelic Realms. You begin to become aware of a wonderful light and energy surrounding you. There is a feeling of a powerful angelic presence in your sanctuary. They are there to provide you with the highest level of healing and empowerment so take some time now to relax and enjoy their wonderful energy and feel it being absorbed into your physical and energetic bodies, renewing and revitalising you and I will return for you shortly. *(Pause for 3 to 4 minutes)*

- It will soon be time to leave your sanctuary so thank your Angels for their healing energies. *(pause for a moment)*
- Now make your way towards the doorway to the stairs knowing that you will carry this beautiful calm energy with you.
- Open the door that leads to the stairwell. Step through the doorway closing the door behind you. Know that this is your own space that you can return to at any time for relaxation, guidance and healing. And keeping that sense of calm and wellbeing, it is time to head back up the stairs.
- So moving back up the stairs on my count,
- 1, 2, 3, breathing slowly and deeply,
- 4, 5, 6, your body is starting to feel heavier
- 7, 8, bringing your awareness back to your physical body,
- 9 and 10, on that top step now and when you're ready, step off the top step.
- **Bringing your awareness completely back to your physical body and this room, your contact with the chair, your feet with the floor. Slowly begin to move your fingers and toes, and in your own time, opening your eyes, fully awake and aware and in the physical world.**

(Watch for them starting to wriggle fingers and toes and keep an eye on anyone who doesn't do this. If a member of the group appears not to want to come back to the room simply repeat the last paragraph, in bold, but raising your voice so that it said slightly louder and firmer. Repeat a third time if necessary moving over to the person and at the end just saying their name and asking that they come back now in to the room, placing your hand gently on their shoulder.)

Spend a few minutes sharing experiences of the meditation. Remember that it's okay if someone fell asleep, could see nothing or did their own thing. If you're keeping a personal journal, you may wish to take some time to record you experience. Don't forget to date the entry.

THEORY: HEALING
The following 'theory' section should be read aloud to the group. You may want to get others to join in and take it in turns to read.

What is Healing?
Today there is a huge array of healing methods from acupuncture to Hopi Ear Candles, Crystal Therapy to Psychic Surgery. For the purpose of our type of work the practise of healing that's referred to is the method of channelling energy through a healer to a recipient, usually through the hands, to help restore harmony and balance. This type of healing may be referred to as 'hands on', 'faith', 'spiritual' or 'Reiki' healing. Whatever it's named, or whichever method is used, ultimately all healers are using the same positive, loving energy. Healing can also be conveyed simply through a touch, a word, a hug or an action, through the act of listening or by being in close proximity to someone who is a powerful healer. Distance or absent healing is also hugely effective and is similar to prayer. The theory is that we are all connected on the spiritual plane through the same universal energy channelled for healing, so one person can direct this energy to another through these connections.

It's a documented fact through various scientifically controlled experiments that people who are sent healing in the form of energy work or prayer feel better and recover quicker than those who aren't, whether they know it's being sent or not. One double-blind randomised trial confirmed that, over a period of 10 months a group of patients in a coronary care unit who were being prayed for, had less severe symptoms, needed less ventilator assistance, antibiotics and diuretics than a group that weren't. (see R.C. Byrd, 'Positive Therapeutic effects of intercessory prayer in a a coronary care unit population', Southern Medical Journal, 1988; 81(7): 826 - 9.)

What's really interesting is that other studies have shown that not only is it irrelevant whether the patients know that they're being sent healing, but it also doesn't seem to matter what their personal beliefs are, or that of the healers. All healing, whatever method, name or doctrine is associated with it, has a profound effect on the physical and psychological state of the patient. (see F. Sicher and E. Targ et al., a randomized double- blind study of the effect of distant healing in a population with advanced AIDS: report on a small scale study' Western Journal of Medicine, 1998; 168(6) 356-63)

So, how does healing work? There's no definitive answer to this question, although there are a number of commonly held theories.

- One theory is that illness is a manifestation of negative thoughts and mental patterns. Healing energy can be used to re-balance the physical, mental, emotional and spiritual aspects of ourselves. A part of the healing process is very often about adopting a more positive outlook, attitude and language. It helps to restore balance and harmony and to promote wholeness and growth in all areas of life.
- Another theory is that illness comes about as a result of blocked chakras and impeded energy flow. Healing works on a subtle level to balance energy flow allowing our bodies, which are naturally self-regulating and self-healing to get on with the job. This is believed to occur on an emotional, mental and spiritual level too.
- It's also said that when something is wrong in our life, whether it's physical, mental, emotional or spiritual, it's because our own energy vibration isn't quite right. By being in the presence of someone with healing energies and receiving a boost of healing energy, our own vibration is corrected or brought back into alignment. This is a phenomenon known as sympathetic vibration. (see glossary)
- Finally, lets not forget, the good old placebo effect, maybe healing helps because a person believes that it will. But in our opinion, that's fine. If placebo is a good benchmark for drugs companies to test medication against, it must have some effect. Never underestimate the power of thought, but that's a whole other book!

We believe that each theory is a potentially valid one and it may well be that a combination of each is the key. We pass on the healing energy, what it does once the person has received it is anybody's guess, we just know that, in our experience it has wonderful effects.

Everyone has healing abilities or can learn them in some form. Some people pray, some are good listeners, others counsel, nurse or actively use 'hands-on' healing methods. Most importantly, we also have the ability to heal ourselves from within.

Healers are a channel, not the source or instigator. Those who appear to be ego-driven or make over-inflated claims about themselves, in our opinion, should be avoided. It's also illegal for anyone other than a trained medical practitioner to diagnose or prescribe.

Although physical contact can be positive, it should also be appropriate and only practised with the client's permission. Healing works just as well with no contact or indeed over distance if necessary. It's not necessary for anyone to remove any clothing in order to receive healing.

When you give healing you should ensure that the person is comfortable, warm and relaxed. It's a good idea that you are in an environment where you will not be disturbed. The recipient can be either seated or lying down. It's good practise to wash your hands before and after giving healing. As well as being hygienic, and disconnects your energy from the client's and disposes of any residual energy that you may have picked up from them.

Before undertaking any healing it's important to ask your Guides for protection to prevent the transfer of any negative emotions or energy. You can also visualise yourself being surrounded by a pure white light or that your hands are being placed through a veil of light.

We always include a time for Absent Healing within our workshops and circle evenings. We feel that in this way we are giving something back in return for the wisdom and knowledge that we receive from Spirit. When we wish well for others with pure intention our own energies are also enhanced as we connect with pure love energy and encourage oneness with the Universal Energy.

We know from personal experiences about the power of healing and in our groups we have had wonderful feedback from many people. It's important to understand however, that healing and curing are not the same thing. For some it's their time to move on towards the spirit realms. Sending healing will help them to tie up loose ends and do so with peace and acceptance.

HELEN & DIANE'S TIPS

- Always check with the recipient that it's okay for you to place your hands on them, if it's not, work in their aura.
- Never act inappropriately. Always keep your hands in the aura when working within the swimsuit area. Recipients should always remain clothed.
- Be aware that it's quite common for some people to get emotional when receiving healing, this is fine, just have some tissues ready. When practising in the group you should all feel that it's a safe environment for this expression without judgement. If someone becomes emotional, simply comfort and reassure them that it's okay. No explanation is necessary.
- If the recipient is lying down, use folded hands towels or cushions in strategic places to ensure comfort. If they're lying on their back, place one under each knee. If they're on their front, place one under each ankle to ensure support.
- Before you start work take a couple of deep breaths to relax and still your mind.
- Begin with your hands in prayer position to focus you intention and connect your energy.
- Ask your Guides to draw close, to help you to channel healing energy and to offer their protection whilst you're working.
- Visualise your connection with the earth, through energy lines extending out from the soles of your feet.
- Then connect with Spirit by visualising a pure white light entering your crown chakra.
- Work intuitively, moving your hands to where you feel they need to be.
- At the end thank your Guides for their assistance.
- When you've finished, ground your energy and ensure that the recipient is grounded before they leave you.
- Don't panic the recipient by attempting to diagnose a physical complaint; this is illegal as well as potentially distressing. Sometimes the feelings in the aura are simply an imbalance in their energy field. Simply make a mental note of the areas that require attention and concentrate on them during the treatment.
- Please remember that if you suspect that you have a medical problem you should always consult your G.P.

PRACTICAL WORK

Read out each exercise, one at a time to the group so that you are all clear as to what you are doing, then allocate a time to complete the exercise.

EXERCISE 1: Scanning the aura

By feeling or 'scanning' someone's aura it's possible to find hot or cold spots, which can indicate an energetic imbalance or sometimes an area of ill health within the physical body. This is a simple skill that develops with practise. It's a good idea to start a healing session by 'scanning' the person's aura for areas that may need more healing than others. Some people are able to see the aura naturally which makes this process quick and easy.

- Make sure that the person is sitting or lying comfortably and place your hands a few inches above their body.
- Start from either the head or the feet and move your hands slowly through their aura until you have covered the entire area of their body.
- You may feel heat, tingling, pulsing or cold areas or you may intuitively know at a certain point that there is an imbalance.
- Discuss your experiences and provide feedback to each other.

EXERCISE 2: Giving healing - working with a partner

- One partner (the recipient) should sit comfortably in a chair.
- The person giving healing should establish a connection with their partner by linking hands or placing your hands on their shoulders for a moment.
- The healer should then follow these instructions.
- Place you hands on the recipient or in their aura wherever you feel that the healing energy is needed
- Ask you Guides to draw close, to help you to channel healing energy and to offer their protection whilst you're working.
- Visualise your connection with the earth, through energy lines extending out from the soles of your feet.
- Then connect with Spirit by visualising a pure white light entering your crown chakra.
- Simply allow the energy to flow through you, leaving through your hands, for a few minutes.
- Stand behind your partner and use the following list of hand positions as a guideline if you wish to or move your hands to were you feel the energy needs to be focussed :
    - Shoulders
    - Top of head
    - Stand to the side of the client
    - One hand on the forehead, the other on the base of the skull
    - One hand on the pit of the throat, the other level with this but on the back of the neck
    - One hand on the breast bone, the other on the back, level with this
    - One hand solar plexus, the other at the same height on the back
    - One hand the lower stomach, the other on the lower back, at the same height
    - Stand in front of the client
    - Both hands on the knees
    - Both hands on the feet
- Discuss your experiences and provide feedback to each other.

EXERCISE 3: Giving healing - working in a group 1 (If you have a massage or treatment couch)
This works in a similar way to working with a partner, except that the recipient receives healing from more than one person. This can be extremely powerful. Ensure that everyone knows that they can ask for the healing to stop at any time if it becomes too much for them.

Here is one example of working in a group:
- With the recipient lying face down on a massage couch or similar you can work on their back.
- Use folded hand towels or cushions in strategic places to ensure comfort. If lying on their back, place under the recipient's knees. If lying on their front, place one under each of their ankles for support.
- The team leader stands at the head with one hand on each of the recipient's shoulders.
- The remaining healers stand at either side and alternate their hands, placing them in a column along the spine.
- A further healer, if there are enough, can remain at the feet.
- Ask your Guides to draw close, to help you to channel healing energy and to offer their protection whilst you're working.
- Visualise your connection with the earth, through energy lines extending out from the soles of your feet.
- Then connect with Spirit by visualising a pure white light entering your crown chakra.
- Hold the positions for as long as required with the intention of allowing energy to flow through you.
- Discuss your experiences and provide feedback to each other.

EXERCISE 4: Giving healing - working in a group 2 (If you have a massage or treatment couch)
A similar method can be used on the front of the body with 3 or 4 healers. Hands should be positioned with care so that the recipient does not feel insecure. Alternatively, place hands in the aura only.
- Use folded hand towels or cushions in strategic places to ensure comfort. If lying on their back, place under the recipient's knees. If lying on their front, place one under each of their ankles for support.
- Healer number one stands at the head, number two to the left, number three to the right and number four at the feet of the recipient.
- Healer number one places their hands either side of the recipient's head.
- Healer number two places one hand below the pit of the throat.
- Healer number three places one hand below the breasts,
- Number two then places their other hand below this and number three below that.
- Ask your Guides to draw close, to help you to channel healing energy and to offer their protection whilst you are working.
- Visualise your connection with the earth, through energy lines extending out from the soles of your feet.
- Then connect with Spirit by visualising a pure white light entering your crown chakra.
- Hold the positions for as long as required with the intention of allowing energy to flow through you.
- Discuss your experiences and provide feedback to each other.

EXERCISE 5: Giving healing - working in a group 3
You can also give healing as a group by using different hand positions that you are drawn to intuitively. You may start with your hands in the positions given in exercise 2 or 3 and then change hand positions during the course of the treatment. You can also do this if you do not have a couch by having the subject seated as in Exercise 1. One person stands behind the chair, one to the left and one to the right.. In order for this to be a relaxing experience for the recipient this may take some forward planning, between the healers involved.
Use the following guidelines:
- Use folded hand towels or cushions in strategic places to ensure comfort. If lying on their back, place under the recipient's knees. If lying on their front, place one under each of their ankles for support.

LESSON FOUR – HEALING

- One person stands behind the chair, or at the head of the couch, one person stands to the left, another to the right. If you have enough healers, an extra person can stand at the feet.
- The person at the head acts as a team leader, indicating with a nod or other non-verbal signal when it's time to change hand positions.
- The team leader should be the first to make contact with the recipient and then indicate to each of the other healers to join in turn.
- Ask your Guides to draw close, to help you to channel healing energy and to offer their protection whilst you're working.
- Visualise your connection with the earth, through energy lines extending out from the soles of your feet.
- Then connect with Spirit by visualising a pure white light entering your crown chakra.
- Work intuitively, moving your hands to where you feel they need to be.
- When it's time to finish it should be indicated by the team leader, and the other healers should gently remove their hands. You can decide intuitively or by timing the healing session.
- The team leader should be the last to remove their hands from the recipient.
- Ensure that everyone has a go at giving and receiving healing.
- Discuss your experiences and provide feedback to each other.

CLOSING & GROUNDING
Once you have completed the exercises and had some discussion time, everyone should sit comfortably and complete the following meditation to close and ground their energy. Read aloud the following: (or use the audio CD.)

- Sit in a comfortable position and close your eyes.
- Bring your attention to your breathing and focus on this for a few breaths. *(Pause)*
- Take your awareness to the invisible energy field surrounding you and visualise it drawing in close around your physical body. *(Pause)*
- Take your awareness to the area just above your crown and see a sphere of light sitting here.
- Imagine that sphere of light shrinking in size until it's tiny, then sinking down through the crown of your head.
- See it slowly descending down past the brow. *(Pause)*
- Into the throat. *(Pause)*
- Then following the line of the spine, down, through your body, towards your heart area. (Pause)
- Down to your solar plexus. *(Pause)*
- Through the abdominal area. *(Pause)*
- To the base of your spine. *(Pause)*
- Now visualise the sphere of energy either leaving through the base of your spine, or dividing in two and sinking down through your legs and leaving through the soles of your feet.
- Feel this energy leaving you and connecting with the earth.
- Have a sense of downward movement, deep in to the earth. *(Pause)*
- Become more aware of your feet and your physical body.
- Let us take a moment to thank our Spirit Guides, Angels and loved ones in Spirit for their presence, protection and wisdom whilst we've been working. Knowing that they will always be on hand should we need to call on them. *(Pause)*
- **Now bring your awareness back to your physical body, the chair you are sitting on and your contact with the floor.**
- **Begin to bring some movement back in to your fingers and toes.**
- **In your own time opening your eyes, fully awake and aware and in the physical world.**

(Watch for them starting to wriggle fingers and toes and keep an eye on anyone who doesn't do this. If a

member of the group appears not to want to come back to the room simply repeat the last three points, in bold, but raising your voice so that it said slightly louder and firmer. Repeat a third time if necessary moving over to the person and at the end just saying their name and asking that they come back into the room now, placing a hand gently on their shoulder.)

Check to ensure that everyone feels grounded before you finish the session. If not, get them to walk around for a little while. Stamping your feet or jumping up and down helps to bring you back to the physical world. If these don't do the trick, you can ground your energy very readily by eating a small amount of food such as a biscuit.

AND ANOTHER THING:
- Read up on alternative therapies and other forms of healing.
- You may wish to try some of them out for yourself – look for taster sessions at psychic fairs and open days.
- Consider taking a course or workshop in healing – Reiki is a particular favourite of ours and with the right teacher can really help you on your spiritual journey too.
- Start your own Absent Healing Book, putting into it the details of anyone who needs some positive energy. Each day, or whenever you can, take the book in your hands and ask your Guides and Angels to join with you to send healing to those listed.

Next Time...
The next lesson will be covering PSYCHOMETRY.
You will need to arrange for the following tools to be brought along:
- Bag with a selection of different colours lengths of ribbon. (You may need more than one if you have a large group.)
- Everyone should bring along a personal possession or an item of jewellery that they wear regularly.
- A bag bowl or box with a cloth to cover, to hold the personal objects

LESSON FIVE
PSYCHOMETRY

PREPARATION
Well in advance of your meeting ensure that you have all of the tools that you require for this lesson. If not, find out if another group member has access to what you need.

Regular tools:
- Healing book
- Pens and pencils
- Paper
- Candles & matches if desired
- Box of tissues

Tools for this lesson:
- Bag with a selection of different colours lengths of ribbon. (You may need more than one if you have a large group.)
- Everyone should bring along a personal possession or an item of jewellery that they wear regularly.
- A bag bowl or box with a cloth to cover, to hold the personal objects

On the day of the meeting ensure that the room is prepared:
Are there enough seats for everyone and enough room for the work you are about to undertake?
Open the windows or burn some incense to freshen the air.
Gather the required tools together. Call and remind anyone who has promised to bring something.
Set out some water and glasses.
Prepare some relaxing background music.

At the beginning of the meeting:
As people arrive ask them to add the names of anyone they know who needs some healing to the Healing Book. Remember that you don't need to put their full names and private information, first names, initials or nicknames will suffice. Whoever you intend to send the healing to, it will reach.

Everyone should place the item of jewellery, or personal object that they have brought, in to a box, bag or bowl with a cloth over it without allowing others to see it.

Once everyone has arrived and is comfortable then you can start.
Work your way through the script and exercises for this lesson as detailed on the following pages.

OPENING & PROTECTION
Read the following script out loud to the group. It's a time of meditation so keep your voice calm and relaxed, reading in a fairly slow and controlled manner. Instructions are in brackets and italics. (Alternatively use the audio CD.)

- Let us take a moment to close our eyes and calm our minds.
- Concentrate on your breathing, allowing the breath to become deeper and slower.

(Pause to allow everyone to take a couple of breaths in and out)

- Let us all mentally ask our Spirit Guides and Angels to draw close and create a circle around our own.
- We let it be known that we are happy to work with Spirit and that we only work in love and light. We ask that anyone from the spirit world who wishes to contact us only does so in love and light and with the highest intentions.
- We ask for your protection, guidance and wisdom as we blend our world with yours. *(Pause)*
- Let us blend and harmonise our energies as we sit together in circle.
- Let us send out a note of harmony to the person on our left. Visualise this as a pale pink mist coming from your heart area and moving towards the heart of the person sitting on your left. *(Pause)*
- As you continue to do this, become aware of receiving the same loving energy from the right.
- As we send and receive this energy, be aware of any changes in the atmosphere within the circle. *(Pause)*
- Have a sense of oneness with the group. *(Pause)*
- Now bring your attention back to yourself and the centre of your being, the lower abdominal area.
- Focus on your breathing; become aware of the rise and fall of your abdomen. As you inhale it will gently rise and as you exhale it will fall. *(Pause to allow everyone to take a few breaths in and out)*
- Have a sense of warmth here and in your mind's eye allow a symbol or shape to form. Imagine that this symbol or shape is sitting at and represents your centre. It may be a simple glow of light, a flame or a flower.
- With each in-breath visualise your symbol becoming larger, stronger or more open whichever is appropriate.
- With each out-breath, imagine that you are exhaling any negativity left from your day, or worries that you may have. *(Pause to allow everyone to take a few breaths in and out)*
- Now take your awareness to the soles of your feet, feeling their contact with the floor. Visualise lines of energy extending out from your feet and down into the ground. In your mind's eye, see these lines of energy as roots extending deep into the earth.
- Earth energy also travels back up through these roots revitalising and nourishing you.
- See this energy entering through the soles of your feet and travelling up through your legs to the base of your spine.
- At the base of the spine imagine that the energy becomes a sphere of deep red mist or light, as you visualise it, it becomes more vibrant in colour. *(Pause)*
- From this point a beam of energy leaves the red sphere and travels up towards the sacral area, just below the belly button. Here it forms a sphere of vibrant orange mist or light. As you focus on it, it becomes stronger in colour. *(Pause)*
- Gradually a beam of energy leaves the orange sphere and travels up towards the solar plexus, where it forms a sphere of clear yellow. With each breath, this yellow becomes stronger and brighter. *(Pause)*
- Once more a beam of energy leaves this sphere and continues its journey up to the heart area. Here a sphere of mist or light begins to form, which you may see as either green or pink. Focus on this area for a few breaths allowing the energy to grow stronger and clearer and to expand. *(Pause)*
- Gradually a beam of energy leaves the heart area and moves upwards to the throat. Here it forms a sphere of clear blue. Once more, as you focus on this area, allow the colour to expand and increase in strength. *(Pause)*
- Now, visualise a strand of energy leaving the throat area and linking with the third eye area, just between and slightly above the eyes. Here energy will begin to form as before. You may see this energy as either a rich indigo or violet, whichever you prefer. Concentrate on this energy and visualise it increasing in strength. *(Pause)*
- Again, a beam of light extends upwards from this area moving to the crown. As it does so, become aware of another beam of energy coming down from above to meet the first. As they meet at the crown a sphere of pure energy begins to form. You may see this energy as either violet or pure white light. This connects you with the higher realms of Spirit.
- As you hold this vision for a few breaths the light grows and strengthens. And as it does so, the beau-

tiful pure light begins to overflow down and around you, surrounding you in its wonderful energy. It fills your aura, cleansing, balancing and strengthening it. You feel safe and comfortable. You feel relaxed and light. *(Longer pause before moving on to the Healing script below.)*

HEALING
- Slowly open your eyes and join hands with those sitting to either side of you. This increases the flow of healing energy.
- We know that our Guides, Angels and loved ones in Spirit have come forward and that they surround us with their healing energies. We ask them to help us as we send out our healing today. *(Pause)*
- Visualise a pool of brilliant white light forming and growing in the middle of our circle. *(Pause)*
- This is a pool of healing energy from which we can all draw when we need to. Know that this universal healing energy will find its way to all of those for whom we request healing.
- We ask for healing for each of us here, for our minds, bodies and spirit.

(If there are absent members: We ask for healing for the members of our group who cannot be with us today.)
- We ask for healing for all of those on our Absent Healing List. Take a moment to visualise them standing the healing pool.
- I would also like to ask for special healing for _____

(Mention anyone else that you feel healing is really important for today. Gently squeeze the hand of the person to your left to indicate that it's their turn. Let everyone have a turn at saying this part before continuing with the script.)
- We send our healing thoughts to Mother Earth and to the plant and animal kingdom. Thank you.
- Release your hands but keep your eyes closed so that you remain relaxed and peaceful as we go in to our meditation. *(Brief pause before moving on to the Meditation script.)*

MEDITATION
- Ensure that you're sitting comfortably with your hands on your knees, palms facing upwards.
- Close your eyes.
- Take a deep inhalation, and breathe out slowly. Continue to breathe slowly and deeply.
- During this meditation you will always be safe and protected, you will feel relaxed and comfortable. If, however, there is anything that does make you feel uneasy, or you wish to come back out of the meditation, you can do so at any time by counting backwards from 3 to 1 and taking a deep breath in and out. You can then bring your awareness back to the physical body, particularly your feet and open your eyes.
- For now though, continue to breathe slowly and deeply, your body feels relaxed and your mind is clear.
- As you breathe images may begin to form in your mind's eye. Don't try to manipulate or analyse them, simply observe them. If you do not automatically see these images, simply imagine or sense them.
- Ahead of you lies a staircase or series of ten steps. Move towards them. At the bottom you can see a doorway. We're going to slowly go down these steps towards the door feeling safe and confident at all times. So moving down the steps on my count:
- 10, 9, 8, with each step feeling lighter and lighter.
- 7, 6, 5, feeling calm and peaceful,
- 4, 3, relaxed and light
- 2 and 1, you find yourself standing in front of the door. Reaching out you open the door and as you do so, a wonderful, warm light shines through from the other side, bathing your whole being in its rays.
- As you stand in this light for a few moments, your physical body is warmed through and your energy body is nourished and energised. This gives you a sense of comfort and completeness and offers further protection on your journey. *(Pause for a short while)*
- Today's journey is designed to help you to extend your senses and to be more sensitive to the type of

- information that can be made available to you by Spirit whilst in an altered state of consciousness.
- The rays of light subside you can see through the doorway to the other side.
- As your eyes adjust to the change in light, colours begin to form shapes. Your sanctuary lies ahead of you and you step through the doorway into your safe place, closing the door behind you.
- In one of the rooms, or an area of your sanctuary you will find a large dining table laid with candles and large bowls. There is also a fire burning in grate or fire pit, if you're outside, with comfortable chairs or places to sit, surrounding it. Make your way to this area and take a seat at the table. Reaching out for the nearest bowl, you find that it's full of large, ripe lemons. Their bright yellow skins glisten in the candlelight. Reach into the bowl and take one of these fruit. Hold the lemon in your hand and feel it's cool firm skin. Trace the outline of the shape of the fruit with your fingers turning it over in your hands. On the table you will also see a plate with a knife placed on it. Take these and use the knife to cut the lemon in half and then into quarters. Feel the sensation of this action coming through the knife and into your hands, see the inside of the lemon and start to smell its aroma drifting up from the cuts. Now take a piece and hold it up to your nose so that you can really smell its strong fragrance. Does it remind you of anything in particular? Does it conjure any images, sensations or memories? Now bite into the sharp fruit, taste the sharp acidic juice and feel your mouth start to water.
- On the table is a jug of water and some cups or glasses, there are also other bowls containing salt, sugar other fruits and nuts. Pour yourself some water, listening to the sound it makes. Drink some to cleanse your palate. Take some time now to experience some of the other items on the table and to see, sense, feel, smell and taste them. You may also wish to sit by the fire in the comfortable armchairs and experience the aroma, sight, sound and warmth of its crackling flames. *(Pause for 5 minutes)*
- It's now time to leave your sanctuary, so make your way towards the doorway to the stairs. Open the door and step through closing it behind you.
- Know that your sanctuary is your own space that you can return to at any time for relaxation, guidance and healing.
- And keeping that sense of calm and wellbeing, it is time to head back up the stairs. So moving back up the stairs on my count,
- 1, 2, 3, breathing slowly and deeply,
- 4, 5, 6, your body is starting to feel heavier
- 7, 8, bringing your awareness back to your physical body,
- 9 and 10, on that top step now and when you're ready, step off the top step.
- **Bringing your awareness completely back to your physical body and this room, your contact with the chair, your feet with the floor. Slowly begin to move your fingers and toes, and in your own time, opening your eyes, fully awake and aware and in the physical world.**

(Watch for them starting to wriggle fingers and toes and keep an eye on anyone who doesn't do this. If a member of the group appears not to want to come back to the room simply repeat the last paragraph, in bold, but raising your voice so that it said slightly louder and firmer. Repeat a third time if necessary moving over to the person and at the end just saying their name and asking that they come back now in to the room, placing your hand gently on their shoulder.)

Spend a few minutes sharing experiences of the meditation. Remember that it's okay if someone fell asleep, could see nothing or did their own thing. If you're keeping a personal journal, you may wish to take some time to record you experience. Don't forget to date the entry.

THEORY: PSYCHOMETRY
The following 'theory' section should be read aloud to the group. You may want to get others to join in and take it in turns to read.

Psychometry is a form of psychic divination using the sense of touch to connect with the energy field of an object in order to 'read' any psychic imprints left by the owner. Such imprints may provide information on a psychic level in the same way that Tarot cards and other divination tools do. It could be likened to being able to feel and translate the fingerprints left by anyone who has touched an object. This imprint is classed as residual energy. Another element of psychometry is that through connecting with the energy of an object, a reader may be able to link to a loved one in Spirit who wishes to make themselves known or pass a message on to the enquirer. These spirits are usually linked in some way with the object, or with the person for whom the reading is being done (or who owns the object).

Many mediums use psychometry as a useful tool to connect with their sitter. By holding an object, for example an item of jewellery that the sitter usually wears, the medium can tap into the sitter's energy field more readily, and thus their thoughts and feelings. By holding a piece of jewellery that belonged to a deceased loved one, a medium may be able to connect to that person's residual energy field, or their spirit, even many years after their death.

Psychic imprints can also be left in an area or building, especially at times of traumatic events. These can be 'read' in the same way. An example of this is when you've perhaps had the experience of walking into a room in which an argument has recently taken place and feeling uncomfortable without initially understanding why. These imprints can, in extreme cases, result in what is known as a residual haunting where events are replayed at regular intervals or significant times. For example, at some historic sites or buildings people report seeing a 'ghost' repeatedly acting in exactly the same way. Some mediums are able to help the police with crime investigations by visiting scenes of crimes and tuning into the residual energy field to find clues. Of course they may also be able to find out further information from holding items connected to the crime.

Psychometry is one of the most basic skills that an aspiring medium can usually master with excellent results. Remember though that as with all things psychic, practise is the key and psychometry skills undoubtedly improve over time.

The most important thing when trying psychometry is to 'give what you get'. As you hold an object in your hands you may find words or images popping into your head that have no meaning or relevance to you. It's important that you simply pass them on to the person whose object you're reading. You may well find that the word or picture is of deep significance to them. If you hold on to the image, feeling or message that you're getting because you feel that it isn't important or that it's silly, you will be blocking yourself. It's like placing your thumb over the end of a hosepipe and not allowing the water to flow. Once you give the information, it's as though you remove your thumb and let the water go, then more will come. As you become more proficient in the art of psychometry, you may find that you receive certain pictures to symbolise other things, e.g. a plane might represent a holiday. However this is something that you will become attuned to with time and practise. In the meantime simply relax and see what you can pick up.

PRACTICAL WORK

Read out each exercise, one at a time to the group so that you are all clear as to what you are doing, then allocate a time to complete the exercise. The first two exercises are to increase your awareness of energy and prepare you for psychometry. However, the only real exercise is to do it. Two different types of psychometry are described in exercises 3 and 4.

EXERCISE 1: Feel the Energy

This exercise will help you to feel and activate the smaller chakras in the hands that will assist you in tuning into and reading the energy of an object.

- Sit comfortably in a chair with your feet flat on the floor.
- Place your palms together and focus your attention on their contact with each other. You may become aware of heat building up.
- After a minute or so separate your hands very slightly. Maintain your focus on the same place between your palms. Very slowly move your hands slightly away from and then towards each other, as though pumping the air between the palms. You should become aware of a feeling of resistance here.
- Gradually take your hands further apart and each time they come back together, still with that pumping action, make the gap between your palms larger and larger. Feel as though there's a ball of energy between your palms. This energy has been created through the smaller chakras in the palms of your hands using your auric energy.
- You can play with the energy with practise. Move your hands around so that you can feel the edges of the ball.
- You will find, in time that this skill has other uses, but for now, it assists you in beginning to feel the auric energy that we talk of and activating the sense of feeling in your hands.

EXERCISE 2: Sensing Colours

You will need a bag of different coloured ribbons.

- Working in pairs, one person closes their eyes.
- The other passes them a ribbon from the bag and should keep notes for their partner.
- Keeping eyes closed, the person receiving the ribbon tries to sense what colour the ribbon is. Be aware of feelings such as 'heavy' or 'soft', 'light' or 'dark' etc. Some people may even be lucky enough to receive an image in their mind, e.g. a sun when holding a yellow coloured ribbon.
- Still with your eyes closed, tell your partner what you get so that they can make a record for you.
- You can try to guess the colour if you want to, although it's just as good to get a sense of how the colour 'feels'.
- Repeat the exercise several times, and then swap round so that you both have a turn at sensing.

EXERCISE 3: Chair Swapping

- Group members should be paired up, and then swap seats with their partner.
- Imagine your aura extending out around you encompassing the energy left behind in this space by your partner.
- Tune into that energy and allow sensations and images to come to you through it. No matter how silly you may think these things it is important to pass them on. Write them down or tell your partner straight away what you're picking up.
- If you have written down the things that you pick up, take some time to give them the information verbally once you feel that you have come to a stop. You may find that as you give them this information more comes to you.

LESSON FIVE - PSYCHOMETRY

EXERCISE 4: Psychometry exercise
- Each person should have already placed their item of jewellery or personal possession into a bag or box/bowl with a cloth over it without allowing others to see it.
- The bowl should be taken round to each person in turn, who, without looking should take one item, ensuring that it's not their own.
- As you hold the item in your hands, extend your senses and tune into the energy of the object. Relax. Feel it's memories, allow images to form in your mind's eye, take note of fragrances, feelings, sensations, words that pop in to your head, sounds that you hear. Don't try to analyse it too much! What are you doing with the object? How are you handling it? This can also mean something to or represent something about the sitter. For example, twisting and turning an object in your hands could indicate that the person is restless, or feels that they are going round in circles with a problem, or it may have been a familiar action of a loved one.
- Sit quietly for a few minutes and write down anything that comes to you.
- After a while these messages will stop and some of you may feel that you know whose item you are holding. Let each person guess at whose they have in their hands, but don't worry if you aren't correct.
- Take time for each person to feed back the information that they have received to the person whose item they have read. Continue to hold the item as you do this as more may come to you as you talk.
- Swap around until everyone has given his or her messages.

When trying psychometry, whether you write down the information as you receive it and feedback to your partner later, or talk them through it straight away, it's a good idea to keep a written record of the messages. They may be validated later, by friends or family members. Your partner may have to check up on it to confirm the details or you may even receive information about a future event.
Remember, this exercise requires practise. Some may find they have a natural ability, but others may not get anything at all on their first attempt.

Now take some time to discuss your experiences as a group. Not necessarily all the messages, but how you found the exercise and how it felt for you.

CLOSING & GROUNDING
Once you have completed the exercises and had some discussion time, everyone should sit comfortably and complete the following meditation to close and ground their energy. Read aloud the following: (or use the audio CD.)

- Sit in a comfortable position and close your eyes.
- Bring your attention to your breathing and focus on this for a few breaths. *(Pause)*
- Take your awareness to the invisible energy field surrounding you and visualise it drawing in close around your physical body. *(Pause)*
- Take your awareness to the area just above your crown and see a sphere of light sitting here.
- Imagine that sphere of light shrinking in size until it's tiny, then sinking down through the crown of your head.
- See it slowly descending down past the brow. *(Pause)*
- Into the throat. *(Pause)*
- Then following the line of the spine, down, through your body, towards your heart area. (Pause)
- Down to your solar plexus. *(Pause)*
- Through the abdominal area. *(Pause)*
- To the base of your spine. *(Pause)*
- Now visualise the sphere of energy either leaving through the base of your spine, or dividing in two and sinking down through your legs and leaving through the soles of your feet.

- Feel this energy leaving you and connecting with the earth.
- Have a sense of downward movement, deep in to the earth. *(Pause)*
- Become more aware of your feet and your physical body.
- Let us take a moment to thank our Spirit Guides, Angels and loved ones in Spirit for their presence, protection and wisdom whilst we've been working. Knowing that they will always be on hand should we need to call on them. *(Pause)*
- **Now bring your awareness back to your physical body, the chair you are sitting on and your contact with the floor.**
- **Begin to bring some movement back in to your fingers and toes.**
- **In your own time opening your eyes, fully awake and aware and in the physical world.**

(Watch for them starting to wriggle fingers and toes and keep an eye on anyone who doesn't do this. If a member of the group appears not to want to come back to the room simply repeat the last three points, in bold, but raising your voice so that it said slightly louder and firmer. Repeat a third time if necessary moving over to the person and at the end just saying their name and asking that they come back into the room now, placing a hand gently on their shoulder.)

Check to ensure that everyone feels grounded before you finish the session. If not, get them to walk around for a little while. Stamping your feet or jumping up and down helps to bring you back to the physical world. If these don't do the trick, you can ground your energy very readily by eating a small amount of food such as a biscuit.

AND ANOTHER THING:
- Practise psychometry on some friends and family.
- Arrange a trip to a local historic house to see if you can feel different energies there.
- A good book to read is 'How To Do Psychic Readings Through Touch' by Ted Andrews

Next Time...
The next lesson will be covering the use of CRYSTALS in our spiritual and psychic work.

To do all of the exercises you will to arrange for the following to be brought along:
- A selection of medium to large tumblestones. If possible, several of each of rose quartz, amethyst, citrine and jasper
- A minimum of 4 clear quartz points
- A selection of small to medium tumblestones for divination: One each of rose quartz, citrine, jasper, haematite, pyrite, clear quartz, sodalite, green aventurine, black tourmaline and tigers eye.
- Discuss with the group if any of you can provide these, or whether you want to invest in them together.

LESSON SIX
CRYSTALS

PREPARATION
Well in advance of your meeting ensure that you have all of the tools that you require for this lesson. If not, find out if another group member has access to what you need.

Regular tools:
- Healing book
- Pens and pencils
- Paper
- Candles & matches if desired
- Box of tissues

Tools for this lesson:
- A selection of medium to large tumblestones. If possible, several of each of rose quartz, amethyst, citrine and jasper
- A minimum of 4 clear quartz points
- A selection of small to medium tumblestones for divination: One each of rose quartz, citrine, jasper, haematite, pyrite, clear quartz, sodalite, green aventurine, black tourmaline and tigers eye.
- Photocopy the required number of the following
    - 'Basic Crystal Information - Handout 8 - enough for one per person

On the day of the meeting ensure that the room is prepared:
Are there enough seats for everyone and enough room for the work you are about to undertake?
Open the windows or burn some incense to freshen the air.
Gather the required tools together. Call and remind anyone who has promised to bring something.
Set out some water and glasses.
Prepare some relaxing background music.

At the beginning of the meeting:
As people arrive ask them to add the names of anyone they know who needs some healing to the Healing Book. Remember that you don't need to put their full names and private information, first names, initials or nicknames will suffice. Whoever you intend to send the healing to, it will reach.

Once everyone has arrived and is comfortable then you can start.
Work your way through the script and exercises for this lesson as detailed on the following pages.

OPENING & PROTECTION
Read the following script out loud to the group. It's a time of meditation so keep your voice calm and relaxed, reading in a fairly slow and controlled manner. Instructions are in brackets and italics. (Alternatively use the audio CD.)

- Let us take a moment to close our eyes and calm our minds.
- Concentrate on your breathing, allowing the breath to become deeper and slower.

(Pause to allow everyone to take a couple of breaths in and out)

- Let us all mentally ask our Spirit Guides and Angels to draw close and create a circle around our own.
- We let it be known that we are happy to work with Spirit and that we only work in love and light. We ask that anyone from the spirit world who wishes to contact us only does so in love and light and with the highest intentions.
- We ask for your protection, guidance and wisdom as we blend our world with yours. *(Pause)*
- Let us blend and harmonise our energies as we sit together in circle.
- Let us send out a note of harmony to the person on our left. Visualise this as a pale pink mist coming from your heart area and moving towards the heart of the person sitting on your left. *(Pause)*
- As you continue to do this, become aware of receiving the same loving energy from the right.
- As we send and receive this energy, be aware of any changes in the atmosphere within the circle. *(Pause)*
- Have a sense of oneness with the group. *(Pause)*
- Now bring your attention back to yourself and the centre of your being, the lower abdominal area.
- Focus on your breathing; become aware of the rise and fall of your abdomen. As you inhale it will gently rise and as you exhale it will fall. *(Pause to allow everyone to take a few breaths in and out)*
- Have a sense of warmth here and in your mind's eye allow a symbol or shape to form. Imagine that this symbol or shape is sitting at and represents your centre. It may be a simple glow of light, a flame or a flower.
- With each in-breath visualise your symbol becoming larger, stronger or more open whichever is appropriate.
- With each out-breath, imagine that you are exhaling any negativity left from your day, or worries that you may have. *(Pause to allow everyone to take a few breaths in and out)*
- Now take your awareness to the soles of your feet, feeling their contact with the floor. Visualise lines of energy extending out from your feet and down into the ground. In your mind's eye, see these lines of energy as roots extending deep into the earth.
- Earth energy also travels back up through these roots revitalising and nourishing you.
- See this energy entering through the soles of your feet and travelling up through your legs to the base of your spine.
- At the base of the spine imagine that the energy becomes a sphere of deep red mist or light, as you visualise it, it becomes more vibrant in colour. *(Pause)*
- From this point a beam of energy leaves the red sphere and travels up towards the sacral area, just below the belly button. Here it forms a sphere of vibrant orange mist or light. As you focus on it, it becomes stronger in colour. *(Pause)*
- Gradually a beam of energy leaves the orange sphere and travels up towards the solar plexus, where it forms a sphere of clear yellow. With each breath, this yellow becomes stronger and brighter. *(Pause)*
- Once more a beam of energy leaves this sphere and continues its journey up to the heart area. Here a sphere of mist or light begins to form, which you may see as either green or pink. Focus on this area for a few breaths allowing the energy to grow stronger and clearer and to expand. *(Pause)*
- Gradually a beam of energy leaves the heart area and moves upwards to the throat. Here it forms a sphere of clear blue. Once more, as you focus on this area, allow the colour to expand and increase in strength. *(Pause)*
- Now, visualise a strand of energy leaving the throat area and linking with the third eye area, just between and slightly above the eyes. Here energy will begin to form as before. You may see this energy as either a rich indigo or violet, whichever you prefer. Concentrate on this energy and visualise it increasing in strength. *(Pause)*
- Again, a beam of light extends upwards from this area moving to the crown. As it does so, become aware of another beam of energy coming down from above to meet the first. As they meet at the crown a sphere of pure energy begins to form. You may see this energy as either violet or pure white light. This connects you with the higher realms of Spirit.
- As you hold this vision for a few breaths the light grows and strengthens. And as it does so, the beau-

tiful pure light begins to overflow down and around you, surrounding you in its wonderful energy. It fills your aura, cleansing, balancing and strengthening it. You feel safe and comfortable. You feel relaxed and light. *(Longer pause before moving on to the Healing script below.)*

HEALING
- Slowly open your eyes and join hands with those sitting to either side of you. This increases the flow of healing energy.
- We know that our Guides, Angels and loved ones in Spirit have come forward and that they surround us with their healing energies. We ask them to help us as we send out our healing today. *(Pause)*
- Visualise a pool of brilliant white light forming and growing in the middle of our circle. *(Pause)*
- This is a pool of healing energy from which we can all draw when we need to. Know that this universal healing energy will find its way to all of those for whom we request healing.
- We ask for healing for each of us here, for our minds, bodies and spirit.

(If there are absent members: We ask for healing for the members of our group who cannot be with us today.)
- We ask for healing for all of those on our Absent Healing List. Take a moment to visualise them standing the healing pool.
- I would also like to ask for special healing for _____

(Mention anyone else that you feel healing is really important for today. Gently squeeze the hand of the person to your left to indicate that it's their turn. Let everyone have a turn at saying this part before continuing with the script.)
- We send our healing thoughts to Mother Earth and to the plant and animal kingdom. Thank you.
- Release your hands but keep your eyes closed so that you remain relaxed and peaceful as we go in to our meditation. *(Brief pause before moving on to the Meditation script.)*

MEDITATION
- Ensure that you're sitting comfortably with your hands on your knees, palms facing upwards.
- Close your eyes.
- Take a deep inhalation, and breathe out slowly. Continue to breathe slowly and deeply.
- During this meditation you will always be safe and protected, you will feel relaxed and comfortable. If, however, there is anything that does make you feel uneasy, or you wish to come back out of the meditation, you can do so at any time by counting backwards from 3 to 1 and taking a deep breath in and out. You can then bring your awareness back to the physical body, particularly your feet and open your eyes.
- For now though, continue to breathe slowly and deeply, your body feels relaxed and your mind is clear.
- As you breathe images may begin to form in your mind's eye. Don't try to manipulate or analyse them, simply observe them. If you do not automatically see these images, simply imagine or sense them.
- Ahead of you lies a staircase or series of ten steps. Move towards them. At the bottom you can see a doorway. We're going to slowly go down these steps towards the door feeling safe and confident at all times. So moving down the steps on my count:
- 10, 9, 8, with each step feeling lighter and lighter.
- 7, 6, 5, feeling calm and peaceful,
- 4, 3, relaxed and light
- 2 and 1, you find yourself standing in front of the door. Reaching out you open the door and as you do so, a wonderful, warm light shines through from the other side, bathing your whole being in its rays.
- As you stand in this light for a few moments, your physical body is warmed through and your energy body is nourished and energised. This gives you a sense of comfort and completeness and offers further protection on your journey. *(Pause for a short while)*
- Today's journey is designed to help you to connect with the energy of Mother Earth.

- The rays of light subside and you can see through the doorway to the other side. You step through the doorway and make your way through your sanctuary to the exit that leads to your garden or outside space. Or your sanctuary may be an outside space.
- You see a path, follow it through your garden or outside space until you get to a gateway, this gateway leads down the side of a cliff, the path is wide and safe and you can see the sea stretching out below you and a beautiful beach at the bottom. Walk through the gateway and follow the path down along the cliff. As you walk you feel happy and content, with the sun on your face and a light breeze.
- When you reach the beach you start to explore. There are lots of cave entrances and you're drawn to one in particular. Looking into the cave it feels slightly cool but you know that it's safe to explore.
- Follow the uneven path into the cave, knowing that you are guided and protected and will find your way easily. Be aware of the smell of the earthy cave. You may hear the sounds of water dripping or a stream running. You may wish to reach out and touch the rocky walls along the way.
- Soon the pathway opens up into a large cavern and as your eyes grow accustomed to the dark you notice the walls and floor of the cavern are gently glistening. Exploring further you can see that there are clumps of crystal growing within the cavern, alongside beautiful structures created by stalactites and stalagmites. Enjoy the cavern and its beautiful architecture by wondering round, touching and absorbing the energy of Mother Earth. Or sit or lie in the middle of the cavern and take in the sights and energy of your surroundings. Feel her warmth, her nurturing energy, the sense of safety. Allow her energy to wash over you as you explore and I will return for you shortly. *(Pause for 5 minutes)*
- It will soon be time to leave your sanctuary. So, feeling nourished and energised and at peace, you make your way back along the cave path that you followed before. As you near the entrance you see the sunlight beginning to stream in. Eventually you emerge into the warmth of the beach. At the entrance to the cave you see a beautiful piece of crystal lying on a rock as though it has been carefully placed there just for you. This is a gift from mother earth for you to cherish. Pick it up, observing its shape and colour, and hold it as you return along the cliff path to the gateway that leads to your garden.
- Go through the gateway and follow the path through the garden to your sanctuary. Enter your sanctuary and find a safe place where you can leave your beautiful crystal so that you see it whenever you wish to return here.
- Open the door that leads to the stairwell. Step through closing the door behind you.
- Know that your sanctuary is your own space that you can return to at any time for relaxation, guidance and healing.
- And keeping that sense of calm and wellbeing, it is time to head back up the stairs. So moving back up the stairs on my count,
- 1, 2, 3, breathing slowly and deeply,
- 4, 5, 6, your body is starting to feel heavier
- 7, 8, bringing your awareness back to your physical body,
- 9 and 10, on that top step now and when you're ready, step off the top step.
- **Bringing your awareness completely back to your physical body and this room, your contact with the chair, your feet with the floor. Slowly begin to move your fingers and toes, and in your own time, opening your eyes, fully awake and aware and in the physical world.**

(Watch for them starting to wriggle fingers and toes and keep an eye on anyone who doesn't do this. If a member of the group appears not to want to come back to the room simply repeat the last paragraph, in bold, but raising your voice so that it said slightly louder and firmer. Repeat a third time if necessary moving over to the person and at the end just saying their name and asking that they come back now in to the room, placing your hand gently on their shoulder.)

Spend a few minutes sharing experiences of the meditation. Remember that it's okay if someone fell asleep, could see nothing or did their own thing. If you're keeping a personal journal, you may wish to take some time to record you experience. Don't forget to date the entry.

LESSON SIX - CRYSTALS

THEORY: CRYSTALS
The following 'theory' section should be read aloud to the group. You may want to get others to join in and take it in turns to read.

Throughout history it has been claimed that crystals are far more than stones or rocks, and that they have metaphysical properties. Each crystal is said to have different properties depending on their make-up and energy. The most common uses referred to by many different cultures are:
- Healing
- Protection
- Courage
- Meditation
- Connecting with the gods
- Manifestation
- Energy work
- Dreamwork
- Astral projection
- Personal / spiritual / psychic development
- Dowsing
- Divination (Lithomancy)

Crystals actually 'grow' in an organised structure. They are created in and of the earth in a variety of ways: in the molten lava and hot gases deep within, or as they pour out of the earth in volcanic areas; in the more superficial layers of the earth or in mineral solutions; under the extreme pressure and high temperatures that occur deep within the earth's crust.

Varying environmental conditions and chemical impurities create the many different crystals within each family of crystal. Their internal geometric structure enables experts to classify the different types of crystal. Different types and amounts of minerals give the crystals their colours, which can vary greatly. Impurities in the crystals create unusual patterns within them, adding to their mystery. Their perfectly uniform structures, combined with their chemical composition and colour give each one its own precise vibration which can often be felt by sensitive individuals.

There are a few different theories about how crystals work
- It's said that when something is wrong in our life, whether it's physical, mental, emotional or spiritual, it's because our own energy vibration isn't quite right. By carrying the right crystal or placing it in our energy field, our vibration is corrected or brought into line with that which we would like to achieve. This is a phenomenon known as sympathetic vibration. (see glossary)
- Crystals, especially quartz magnify energy so they can be used in combination with healing in order to intensify the healing effects on the recipient.
- Crystals are said to radiate their own healing energy in a powerful and concentrated way, much like a 'laser beam'. This can be directed to a specific point where pain, imbalance or disease occurs in order to treat it.
- Another theory is that crystals have a placebo effect and work to facilitate healing because a person believes that they will.

We believe that each theory is a potentially valid one and it may well be that if crystals do indeed have metaphysical properties, an element from each of them could be playing their part. We would suggest that if you want to try them out, do so with an open mind. If you find that crystals are of benefit to you, fantastic! Then decide whether it's important to know how they work or if you can just accept that they do. (Please remember that if you suspect that you have a medical problem you should always consult a G.P.)

There are plenty of books and references to crystals and their uses, however, it's really best to allow your intuition to pick the right one for you. Find somewhere selling crystals and see which one you're most drawn to. Let your crystal pick you! Keep in mind your specific purpose, or ask, in your mind, that you find the one that's best for you at this moment in time. You may find that by holding them, one feels warm or as though it has a pulse. You could be surprised at the physical reactions and sensations that you receive when handling crystals. Don't try too hard though, even if you pick a crystal simply because you like the colour, it'll be the one that you should have. You can also intuitively choose crystals for friends by thinking of the person in question and again, seeing which crystal you feel drawn to for them. Additionally if you're ever buying crystals for yourself and feel compelled to buy one for a specific friend, then do so, there'll be a reason for it. Start with small tumblestones that you can put in your pocket and keep close to you. These are fairly inexpensive too, so you can try them out without spending much. Our guide to 'Basic Crystal Information' (Handout 8) will give you a starting point.

The first thing that you should always do with a new crystal is to cleanse it, although you should find out a bit about them first as some can't be cleansed in water. Cleansing is done to shift any energy left by those who have handled it before or absorbed by the crystal from its previous surroundings. Cleansing can be done in a number of ways. It can be held in a flowing stream out in nature, or even under the tap, asking that any negativities be washed away and recycled by the earth into positive energies. You can bury them in a pot of soil or salt (preferably rock salt) or in the garden. Or they can be left in salt water for a few hours. Alternatively, you could simply hold it in your hands asking for it to be cleansed or visualise a cleansing pure white light around it.

Once you've cleansed the crystal you can then dedicate it to serve a specific purpose. For example to help you give up smoking, to help with arthritis and so on. You may simply have been drawn to buy a crystal or not know why a friend has specifically given you it. In these cases you may wish to not dedicate it for any one thing, this is fine too.

You should try to recharge your crystals regularly. This can easily be achieved by leaving them in the sunlight, moonlight or rain for a few hours (again, beware of porous crystals that will disintegrate in water). Crystals love thunderstorms and seem to be especially charged up after being left outside during one.

What you do with crystals generally depends on the type, size and shape of them. This is a very basic starting point for you:
- Crystal pendants and other jewellery are a great way to carry crystal energy with you wherever you go.
- Tumblestones can be put in a small pouch and kept in a pocket or handbag. They're used for healing, energy work or divination.
- Crystal balls look great as an ornament, are used for scrying and will enhance the energy of a room.
- Natural points or shaped wands are specifically used for healing and chakra work.
- Pendulums can be used for healing, chakra work and dowsing.
- Clusters, caves and geodes are often used for decorative purposes. They radiate positive energy into and absorb negative energy from their environment. Also, they're said to be good for cleansing or could be used as a focus during meditation.

LESSON SIX - CRYSTALS

PRACTICAL WORK
Read out each exercise, one at a time to the group so that you are all clear as to what you are doing, then allocate a time to complete the exercise.

EXERCISE 1: Feeling
- For this exercise you will need several of each of the following crystals preferably in the form of medium sized tumblestones: rose quartz, amethyst, citrine, and jasper.
- You can work as one large group if you have enough crystals, or divided into smaller groups.
- Everyone in the group holds the same type of crystal. As you hold it between the palms of your hands, relax and see how the crystal makes you feel. You may feel something physical, a feeling or a sensation around a particular chakra. You may also see colours or images in your mind's eye.
- Make a note of what you get.
- After you have all held the first type of crystal, try the exercise with another type of crystal. How does it make you feel? How does it differ from the first crystal?
- Repeat until you have worked with each of the crystals.
- At the end compare notes. Did you have similar sensations?

EXERCISE 2: Wheeling
- Create a circle shape with a minimum of four clear quartz points. Ensure that all of the points are pointing in a clockwise direction around the circle.
- Take it in turns to stand or lie in the crystal circle. Be aware that you may find yourself swaying in the crystal circle so the rest of the group will want to keep an eye on you and steady you if required. Whilst in the circle, relax and feel the energies from the clear quartz.
- When you've all had a go in the circle, you can change the exercise by turning the points so that they all face inwards. See how it changes the energies when you step back into the circle.
- You can change it again by pointing all the crystals away from the centre of the circle.
- If you have enough of right sort of crystals you can also perform this exercise with amethyst or other points to compare how this changes the experience.

EXERCISE 3: Reading
- You will need a selection of small-medium crystal tumblestones laid out on a table or in a box. We would suggest: amethyst, rose quartz, citrine, jasper, haematite, pyrite, clear quartz, sodalite, green aventurine, black tourmaline and tigers eye.
- Take it in turns to pick a crystal. Try not to spend too long choosing your crystal, instead pick the one that you feel most drawn to, even if you're drawn to it simply because you like its colour or shape!
- Look at the 'Basic Crystal Information' handout and think about why you have been drawn to it. Consider its colour too, and which chakra it might relate to. Replace the crystal before the next person chooses theirs, so that everyone picks from the full selection.
- Repeat the exercise, but this time choose the crystal that you like the least. Again look at its attributes and think about why you do not feel comfortable with it.
- Keep a record of your findings.

EXERCISE 4: Cleansing
- Take two cups of tap water (use tap water rather than filtered or bottled water).
- Put a clear quartz crystal into one of the cups and leave it for at least five minutes.
- Remove the quartz and then taste both cups of water. Can you taste any difference between the two?
- Clear quartz is an excellent purifying crystal, and can alter the taste of tap water, sometimes quite dramatically.
- Discuss your thoughts in the group.

CLOSING & GROUNDING

Once you have completed the exercises and had some discussion time, everyone should sit comfortably and complete the following meditation to close and ground their energy. Read aloud the following: (or use the audio CD.)

- Sit in a comfortable position and close your eyes.
- Bring your attention to your breathing and focus on this for a few breaths. *(Pause)*
- Take your awareness to the invisible energy field surrounding you and visualise it drawing in close around your physical body. *(Pause)*
- Take your awareness to the area just above your crown and see a sphere of light sitting here.
- Imagine that sphere of light shrinking in size until it's tiny, then sinking down through the crown of your head.
- See it slowly descending down past the brow. *(Pause)*
- Into the throat. *(Pause)*
- Then following the line of the spine, down, through your body, towards your heart area. (Pause)
- Down to your solar plexus. *(Pause)*
- Through the abdominal area. *(Pause)*
- To the base of your spine. *(Pause)*
- Now visualise the sphere of energy either leaving through the base of your spine, or dividing in two and sinking down through your legs and leaving through the soles of your feet.
- Feel this energy leaving you and connecting with the earth.
- Have a sense of downward movement, deep in to the earth. *(Pause)*
- Become more aware of your feet and your physical body.
- Let us take a moment to thank our Spirit Guides, Angels and loved ones in Spirit for their presence, protection and wisdom whilst we've been working. Knowing that they will always be on hand should we need to call on them. *(Pause)*
- **Now bring your awareness back to your physical body, the chair you are sitting on and your contact with the floor.**
- **Begin to bring some movement back in to your fingers and toes.**
- **In your own time opening your eyes, fully awake and aware and in the physical world.**

(Watch for them starting to wriggle fingers and toes and keep an eye on anyone who doesn't do this. If a member of the group appears not to want to come back to the room simply repeat the last three points, in bold, but raising your voice so that it said slightly louder and firmer. Repeat a third time if necessary moving over to the person and at the end just saying their name and asking that they come back into the room now, placing a hand gently on their shoulder.)

Check to ensure that everyone feels grounded before you finish the session. If not, get them to walk around for a little while. Stamping your feet or jumping up and down helps to bring you back to the physical world. If these don't do the trick, you can ground your energy very readily by eating a small amount of food such as a biscuit.
of food such as a biscuit.

AND ANOTHER THING:

- Why not visit a shop that sells crystals (or a friend with a collection) and see what you pick up? Which ones are you drawn to and why? Do a bit of research on these and see what the books have to say on them. You may find that there's a reason for you being drawn to them. You may also find that you want to start a collection of your own and do a bit more research in to the subject. If you buy a crystal, take it home, cleanse and dedicate it as detailed earlier in this lesson, and work with it on a daily basis, even if you simply carry it around with you. The more work that you do with crys-

LESSON SIX - CRYSTALS

tals the more sensitive you'll be to their wonderful energies.
- We would recommend 'The Crystal Bible' by Judy Hall. It's a great book that is simple to understand and has lots of pictures and information.
- Experiment with holding different crystals and tuning into their energies, how do they make you feel, what colours, sensations or images do they invoke?
- Why not try lying down with the appropriate coloured crystals on your body at the chakras points? This can provide a powerful experience.
- Try giving crystal readings (this is called lithomancy) by placing a mixture of tumblestones in a bag and having a partner pull out three or four. What do they 'say' to you? You may start using the 'Basic Crystal Information' handout, or another reference guide or book, but you will soon get to know the crystals and what they represent, and perhaps be able to use your intuition to read them too.

Next Time...
The next lesson will be covering DOWSING.
You will need to arrange for the following tools to be brought along:
- Pendulums and / or copper rods for the practical work

LESSON SEVEN
DOWSING

PREPARATION
Well in advance of your meeting ensure that you have all of the tools that you require for this lesson. If not, find out if another group member has access to what you need.

Regular tools:
- Healing book
- Pens and pencils
- Paper
- Candles & matches if desired
- Box of tissues

Tools for this lesson:
- One or more pendulum
- One or more pairs of copper rods
- Photocopy the required number of the following handouts:
    - 'Basic Chakras Information' - Handout 3 - enough for one per person
    - 'Body / Chakras Outline' - Handout 4 - enough for 1-2 per person
    - 'Basic Colour Information' - Handout 5 - enough for one per person
    - 'Pendulum Colour Charts' - Handout 6 - enough for one per person

On the day of the meeting ensure that the room is prepared:
Are there enough seats for everyone and enough room for the work you are about to undertake?
Open the windows or burn some incense to freshen the air.
Gather the required tools together. Call and remind anyone who has promised to bring something.
Set out some water and glasses.
Prepare some relaxing background music.

At the beginning of the meeting:
As people arrive ask them to add the names of anyone they know who needs some healing to the Healing Book. Remember that you don't need to put their full names and private information, first names, initials or nicknames will suffice. Whoever you intend to send the healing to, it will reach.

Once everyone has arrived and is comfortable then you can start.
Work your way through the script and exercises for this lesson as detailed on the following pages.

OPENING & PROTECTION
Read the following script out loud to the group. It's a time of meditation so keep your voice calm and relaxed, reading in a fairly slow and controlled manner. Instructions are in brackets and italics. (Alternatively use the audio CD.)

- Let us take a moment to close our eyes and calm our minds.
- Concentrate on your breathing, allowing the breath to become deeper and slower.

(Pause to allow everyone to take a couple of breaths in and out)

- Let us all mentally ask our Spirit Guides and Angels to draw close and create a circle around our own.
- We let it be known that we are happy to work with Spirit and that we only work in love and light. We ask that anyone from the spirit world who wishes to contact us only does so in love and light and with the highest intentions.
- We ask for your protection, guidance and wisdom as we blend our world with yours. *(Pause)*
- Let us blend and harmonise our energies as we sit together in circle.
- Let us send out a note of harmony to the person on our left. Visualise this as a pale pink mist coming from your heart area and moving towards the heart of the person sitting on your left. *(Pause)*
- As you continue to do this, become aware of receiving the same loving energy from the right.
- As we send and receive this energy, be aware of any changes in the atmosphere within the circle. *(Pause)*
- Have a sense of oneness with the group. *(Pause)*
- Now bring your attention back to yourself and the centre of your being, the lower abdominal area.
- Focus on your breathing; become aware of the rise and fall of your abdomen. As you inhale it will gently rise and as you exhale it will fall. *(Pause to allow everyone to take a few breaths in and out)*
- Have a sense of warmth here and in your mind's eye allow a symbol or shape to form. Imagine that this symbol or shape is sitting at and represents your centre. It may be a simple glow of light, a flame or a flower.
- With each in-breath visualise your symbol becoming larger, stronger or more open whichever is appropriate.
- With each out-breath, imagine that you are exhaling any negativity left from your day, or worries that you may have. *(Pause to allow everyone to take a few breaths in and out)*
- Now take your awareness to the soles of your feet, feeling their contact with the floor. Visualise lines of energy extending out from your feet and down into the ground. In your mind's eye, see these lines of energy as roots extending deep into the earth.
- Earth energy also travels back up through these roots revitalising and nourishing you.
- See this energy entering through the soles of your feet and travelling up through your legs to the base of your spine.
- At the base of the spine imagine that the energy becomes a sphere of deep red mist or light, as you visualise it, it becomes more vibrant in colour. *(Pause)*
- From this point a beam of energy leaves the red sphere and travels up towards the sacral area, just below the belly button. Here it forms a sphere of vibrant orange mist or light. As you focus on it, it becomes stronger in colour. *(Pause)*
- Gradually a beam of energy leaves the orange sphere and travels up towards the solar plexus, where it forms a sphere of clear yellow. With each breath, this yellow becomes stronger and brighter. *(Pause)*
- Once more a beam of energy leaves this sphere and continues its journey up to the heart area. Here a sphere of mist or light begins to form, which you may see as either green or pink. Focus on this area for a few breaths allowing the energy to grow stronger and clearer and to expand. *(Pause)*
- Gradually a beam of energy leaves the heart area and moves upwards to the throat. Here it forms a sphere of clear blue. Once more, as you focus on this area, allow the colour to expand and increase in strength. *(Pause)*
- Now, visualise a strand of energy leaving the throat area and linking with the third eye area, just between and slightly above the eyes. Here energy will begin to form as before. You may see this energy as either a rich indigo or violet, whichever you prefer. Concentrate on this energy and visualise it increasing in strength. *(Pause)*
- Again, a beam of light extends upwards from this area moving to the crown. As it does so, become aware of another beam of energy coming down from above to meet the first. As they meet at the crown a sphere of pure energy begins to form. You may see this energy as either violet or pure white light. This connects you with the higher realms of Spirit.
- As you hold this vision for a few breaths the light grows and strengthens. And as it does so, the beau-

tiful pure light begins to overflow down and around you, surrounding you in its wonderful energy. It fills your aura, cleansing, balancing and strengthening it. You feel safe and comfortable. You feel relaxed and light. *(Longer pause before moving on to the Healing script below.)*

HEALING
- Slowly open your eyes and join hands with those sitting to either side of you. This increases the flow of healing energy.
- We know that our Guides, Angels and loved ones in Spirit have come forward and that they surround us with their healing energies. We ask them to help us as we send out our healing today. *(Pause)*
- Visualise a pool of brilliant white light forming and growing in the middle of our circle. *(Pause)*
- This is a pool of healing energy from which we can all draw when we need to. Know that this universal healing energy will find its way to all of those for whom we request healing.
- We ask for healing for each of us here, for our minds, bodies and spirit.

(If there are absent members: We ask for healing for the members of our group who cannot be with us today.)
- We ask for healing for all of those on our Absent Healing List. Take a moment to visualise them standing the healing pool.
- I would also like to ask for special healing for _____

(Mention anyone else that you feel healing is really important for today. Gently squeeze the hand of the person to your left to indicate that it's their turn. Let everyone have a turn at saying this part before continuing with the script.)
- We send our healing thoughts to Mother Earth and to the plant and animal kingdom. Thank you.
- Release your hands but keep your eyes closed so that you remain relaxed and peaceful as we go in to our meditation. *(Brief pause before moving on to the Meditation script.)*

MEDITATION
- Ensure that you're sitting comfortably with your hands on your knees, palms facing upwards.
- Close your eyes.
- Take a deep inhalation, and breathe out slowly. Continue to breathe slowly and deeply.
- During this meditation you will always be safe and protected, you will feel relaxed and comfortable. If, however, there is anything that does make you feel uneasy, or you wish to come back out of the meditation, you can do so at any time by counting backwards from 3 to 1 and taking a deep breath in and out. You can then bring your awareness back to the physical body, particularly your feet and open your eyes.
- For now though, continue to breathe slowly and deeply, your body feels relaxed and your mind is clear.
- As you breathe images may begin to form in your mind's eye. Don't try to manipulate or analyse them, simply observe them. If you do not automatically see these images, simply imagine or sense them.
- Ahead of you lies a staircase or series of ten steps. Move towards them. At the bottom you can see a doorway. We're going to slowly go down these steps towards the door feeling safe and confident at all times. So moving down the steps on my count:
- 10, 9, 8, with each step feeling lighter and lighter.
- 7, 6, 5, feeling calm and peaceful,
- 4, 3, relaxed and light
- 2 and 1, you find yourself standing in front of the door. Reaching out you open the door and as you do so, a wonderful, warm light shines through from the other side, bathing your whole being in its rays.
- As you stand in this light for a few moments, your physical body is warmed through and your energy body is nourished and energised. This gives you a sense of comfort and completeness and offers further protection on your journey. *(Pause for a short while)*
- Today's journey is designed to help you to connect with the energy of Air.

- The rays of light subside and you can now see through the doorway to the other side.
- You step through the doorway and make your way through your sanctuary to the exit that leads to your garden or outside space or you may already be outside.
- You find yourself on a path that leads you through your beautiful garden or outside space. Follow this path and enjoy the scenery as you walk. You are surrounded by wonderful plants and trees. Notice the colours and the scents. Finally you reach a gateway, which gives you access to a cliff path. You can follow it down to the beach or up to the cliff tops. The path is wide and safe. It's up to you which way you venture.
- Walk through the gateway and follow whichever path you feel drawn to. As you walk you feel happy and content. It's warm and you can feel a gentle breeze against your skin and in your hair.
- When you reach your destination, either the beautiful beach or the wilder cliff tops, take some time to look out to sea. Here you can see the affect of so many different elements of Mother Nature. The wind, the pull of the moon, the nature of the seabed, whether it is smooth or rocky all contribute to the patterns that you see forming in the ocean, from the smooth patches of water to the ripples, from the rolling seas to the crashing waves. *(Pause)*
- Looking up to the sky above you, you can see clouds being whisked along by breezes in the atmosphere. You may not be able to see the air as such, but you can see and feel it's affects. Tune in now to this powerful element, knowing that you are safe and protected in this place. Feel and watch the energy of air around you in different aspects of nature, the sea, the sky, the birds, or trees. Feel it energise you. Feel a part of it. Enjoy this experience and I will return for you shortly. *(Pause for 5 minutes)*
- It is now time to head back to your sanctuary. So, feeling energised and refreshed, you make your way back along the cliff path that you followed before. Along your way you will find an object lying on the ground. This object is connected with the element of air and has been placed here, on a breeze, just for you. Pick it up, observing its shape and colour, and hold it as you return along the cliff path to the gateway that leads to your garden.
- Go through the gateway and follow the path through your garden to your sanctuary. Enter your sanctuary and find a safe place where you can leave your beautiful gift so that you see it whenever you wish to return here. If you have received other gifts during past meditations, you may wish to keep them all together in the same place in your sanctuary.
- Open the door that leads to the stairwell. Step through closing the door behind you.
- Know that your sanctuary is your own space that you can return to at any time for relaxation, guidance and healing.
- And keeping that sense of calm and wellbeing, it is time to head back up the stairs. So moving back up the stairs on my count,
- 1, 2, 3, breathing slowly and deeply,
- 4, 5, 6, your body is starting to feel heavier
- 7, 8, bringing your awareness back to your physical body,
- 9 and 10, on that top step now and when you're ready, step off the top step.
- **Bringing your awareness completely back to your physical body and this room, your contact with the chair, your feet with the floor. Slowly begin to move your fingers and toes, and in your own time, opening your eyes, fully awake and aware and in the physical world.**

(Watch for them starting to wriggle fingers and toes and keep an eye on anyone who doesn't do this. If a member of the group appears not to want to come back to the room simply repeat the last paragraph, in bold, but raising your voice so that it said slightly louder and firmer. Repeat a third time if necessary moving over to the person and at the end just saying their name and asking that they come back now in to the room, placing your hand gently on their shoulder.)

Spend a few minutes sharing experiences of the meditation. Remember that it's okay if someone fell asleep, could see nothing or did their own thing. If you're keeping a personal journal, you may wish to take some time to record you experience. Don't forget to date the entry.

THEORY: DOWSING
The following 'theory' section should be read aloud to the group. You may want to get others to join in and take it in turns to read.

Dowsing is the practise of using a device such as a stick, L-shaped rods or a pendulum to find a person place or thing, or the answers to questions, indicated by the device's movements.

The more traditional or commonly thought-of form of dowsing is the use of a Y-shaped hazel rod to find (divine for) underground water. There are many stories and documented cases of dowsing successes throughout history from locating the best place to sink wells, attempts to find oil and even to determining the sex of an unborn baby: the 'ring-on-a-string-over-the-bump' thing! There have also been many attempts both to discredit dowsing and to seek an explanation as to how it works. As with most of these subjects, there's no definitive answer as to how dowsing works, only theories. Remain open-minded, try it for yourself, then decide whether you need to know how it works, or if you can simply accept that it does.

Dowsing is either about tuning into a particular energy in order to locate its source or about finding out information. One theory on how this discipline works is that there's a massive pool of collective information in the universe and that a part of our mind, which is usually untapped, is able to link in to this and 'know', 'find' or 'remember' the information that's required. Then tiny, imperceptible, muscular movements cause the dowsing device to move in the required manner to provide the correct information to our conscious mind.

Of course, in theory, this means that we shouldn't need a pendulum or other tool at all. Again, as with many of these subjects, if our abilities are finely-tuned we can work without the tools, however they do provide a starting point, something to focus on as well as a clear visual guide to the answers.

It also means that we have to be careful to remain detached as we can often influence the answers that are given. If you're seeking answers to something that you have strong feelings about it might be wise for someone else to dowse for you.

You can dowse to find the location of an object or similar by walking around an area or by holding your rods or pendulum over a map or drawing. Focus your attention on the energy of the object you are seeking. Have a picture in your mind or recall how it smells or makes you feel. Rods or a pendulum will move to indicate the objects whereabouts. Practise will allow you to translate your device's movements. Bear in mind that movements and their translated meanings can vary hugely from one person to the next so you must work it out for yourself.

If you find that you have a knack for dowsing, don't be put off if someone says that they saw your hand move or that they think you are moving the device yourself – the answer to this is that you are, but subconsciously. Ask that they judge your results rather than your methods. Then get them to have a go and experience it for themselves.

PRACTICAL WORK
Read out each exercise, one at a time to the group so that you are all clear as to what you are doing, then allocate a time to complete the exercise.

The most common methods of dowsing are using copper rods or a pendulum. We've already used pendulums for some of the practical work in previous lessons so you should feel comfortable with these. You may want to stick with them or challenge yourself by using the rods, it's up to you. Some people work well with one tool and find the other just does nothing for them. There are a couple of repeated exercises from previous lessons. All of these subjects are very linked so there's often a cross over with the exercises. It can be interesting to see how you have progressed when you revisit these.

EXERCISE 1: Orientation
- Usually rods cross each other to indicate a positive but still do this exercise as it may be different for you. A pendulum may spin clockwise or anti-clockwise, go back and forth or sideways, or even do nothing at all. We always establish orientation before beginning dowsing on every occasion to ensure accuracy.
- To establish the direction of movement or the response that indicates 'yes' and 'no', start by holding the rods or pendulum in a firm but relaxed manner. If using a pendulum, hold it in your dominant hand. You can place your other hand an inch or two below it. It seems that this creates some sort of circuit between the pendulum and us, making it easier to use. Experiment doing this exercise with and without your hand underneath it to see if it makes a difference for you.
- Now either ask for it to move to indicate 'yes' or ask a question to which you know the answer is positive, for example, "Am I a female?" Note the movement of the device and then say "Thank you" or "Stop"
- Repeat this for a 'no' response. Then ask it stop or say 'Thank You' once more.

EXERCISE 2: Yes or No?
- Once you have established the orientation of your pendulum or rods you can start to ask questions of them. This exercise will get you practised at it.
- Working in pairs, decide who will be the first dowser. The other person (the enquirer) should write a question and the answer on a piece of paper, (stick to yes / no answers for now) fold it up and place it in a pocket or somewhere out of view. It should be something that they know their partner does not know the answer to, such as "Did I have toast for breakfast?" followed by 'yes' or 'no'.
- The enquirer should then ask the dowser the question and allow them to dowse for the answer. You may want to try two or three questions then swap over and repeat the exercise the other way round.
- Keep a written record of your results

EXERCISE 3: More Info
- Now try dowsing for more detailed information.
- Working in pairs, take it in turns to do this. As an example, dowse for the colour and type of your partners front door, provided you do not know of course. If you do, come up with something else.
- You will have to be specific and ask questions such as, 'Is the door UPVC?' 'Is the door wooden?' 'Is the door painted?' etc. before you even get on to the colours. See if you can build up a picture.
- Your partner can take notes on your behalf.
- When you think that you have enough information to narrow it down to an answer, tell your partner and discuss your results.
- Swap over so that you both get a go.

LESSON SEVEN - DOWSING

EXERCISE 4: Dowsing the Chakras
- Hand out the 'Body / Chakras Outline' handout.
- Working in threes, one person (the subject) lays with their back on the floor or a couch.
- The second person holds the pendulum in the subject's aura at the feet but in line with their spine. Allow the pendulum to hang free about 1-2 inches above their physical body. From here, slowly draw the pendulum along the mid-line of the body.
- You may feel the pendulum dragging through the auric energy at certain points and it may even appear to stop. If you feel that you want to pause, then pause. The key with this exercise is to use your intuition. At the chakras it will usually pause and either spin or make crossways movements.
- The third person can observe and record the movements of the pendulum using the 'Body / Chakras Outline' handout.
- If the pendulum spins it indicates that the chakra's energy is flowing well.
- However, if it spins widely, it can indicate that the chakra is too open. This may indicate that the person needs to be more protective of their energy as they may be losing energy to others or to the ether for some reason. The reasons will depend on which chakra is affected.
- If the pendulum spins but in a very small, tight, circle it can indicate that the chakra is too closed. Again the reasons depend on the chakra.
- If the pendulum does not move at all, this can also suggest that the chakra is not open enough.
- If the pendulum criss-crosses, let it continue to do so until it begins to spin. This can take some time and indicates that there is an energy blockage. The pendulum will work to free up the blockage and allow the energy to flow as it should. Reasons for this are similar to those when chakras are too closed.
- Refer to 'Basic Chakras Information to analyse your results.
- Swap around so that everyone gets the opportunity to try this exercise as the subject, dowser and observer.

EXERCISE 5: Auras
- Working in pairs use a pendulum or dowsing rods and take it in turns to divine for the edge of each other's auras.
- The subject should stand in the middle of the room while you, starting from as far away as you can, slowly walk towards them with your rods or pendulum.
- Focus your mind on finding their aura and you will at some point get a reaction from your dowsing device.
- Try this exercise again but ask your partner to either expand or withdraw their aura - not telling you which they're doing. See what you discover and discuss your results.
- Swap around so that everyone gets a chance to try this exercise.

EXERCISE 6: Colours
- You will need the 'Pendulum Colour Charts'. We have provided two different charts, you may wish to colour them as appropriate to help you tune into the colours. Practise this exercise with both charts and find the one that works best for you. You will also need at least one pendulum.
- Holding the pendulum with one hand take a couple of breaths and ask that the pendulum moves to indicate 'YES'. It should slowly begin to move in a particular way, sideways, back & forth or in a clockwise or anticlockwise circle. Make a note of this then ask it to move to indicate 'NO', wait for the movement and make a note of it. Ask it to 'STOP' or say 'THANK YOU'.
- Now ask the pendulum to show you which colour(s) you are mainly vibrating in at the moment. Hold the pendulum over each colour in turn, and see how it moves.
- Now repeat the exercise asking which colour(s) you are most lacking in.
- You can also ask the pendulum to show you which colours you would most benefit from at the present time.
- Make notes of your findings and refer to the 'Basic Colour Information' to analyse them.

EXERCISE 7: Futuristic
- If a member of the group or a partner is pregnant why not try dowsing for the sex, weight and birth date of the baby? Keep a record of everyone's answers and see who gets the best results.
- Each member of the group should write one or two questions regarding future events or the outcome of a particular scenario. They can either dowse for the answers or ask other members of the group to do so. Keep a written and dated record of them. It'll be interesting for you to come back to these notes in the future and see how accurate you are.

EXERCISE 8: Location
- These methods can be used to find the location of a lost item or to establish lines of earth energy (Ley Lines), underground streams or the source of water.
- You can practise this in a number of ways. Start by having one person hide an object somewhere within just one room or a defined outside space and see who gets the closest to it.
- You can either dowse by walking around the area or by holding your rods or pendulum over a map or drawing.
- Hold the rods or pendulum firmly but in a relaxed manner.
- Relax your body and take a few deep breaths.
- Focus your mind on the item for which you are searching or the energy of it and ask your Guides to assist in finding it. The movement of the tools you are using will help to indicate which direction you should be looking in. When working in this way, it is impossible for us to tell you what to expect or how it will work for you, as it can be very different for everyone, although, rods usually cross each other to indicate that they're picking up on the energy in question. With practise you will get used to how they work for and 'speak' to you.
- If you're using a map or drawing, another method is to divide it into segments, perhaps by drawing a grid over it in pencil. You can then ask if the item is in each segment in turn, narrowing it down each time you get a 'no'.
- Next you could try hiding an object anywhere in a house so that the dowsers have a larger area to search. All have a go at trying to work out where the item is and, when you think you know, write it down on a piece of paper and give it to the person who hid it. When everyone is finished see who got the closest.
- Discuss the different methods used by the dowsers and see what you learn from each other.

CLOSING & GROUNDING
Once you have completed the exercises and had some discussion time, everyone should sit comfortably and complete the following meditation to close and ground their energy. Read aloud the following: (or use the audio CD.)

- Sit in a comfortable position and close your eyes.
- Bring your attention to your breathing and focus on this for a few breaths. *(Pause)*
- Take your awareness to the invisible energy field surrounding you and visualise it drawing in close around your physical body. *(Pause)*
- Take your awareness to the area just above your crown and see a sphere of light sitting here.
- Imagine that sphere of light shrinking in size until it's tiny, then sinking down through the crown of your head.
- See it slowly descending down past the brow. *(Pause)*
- Into the throat. *(Pause)*
- Then following the line of the spine, down, through your body, towards your heart area. (Pause)
- Down to your solar plexus. *(Pause)*
- Through the abdominal area. *(Pause)*

LESSON SEVEN - DOWSING

- To the base of your spine. *(Pause)*
- Now visualise the sphere of energy either leaving through the base of your spine, or dividing in two and sinking down through your legs and leaving through the soles of your feet.
- Feel this energy leaving you and connecting with the earth.
- Have a sense of downward movement, deep in to the earth. *(Pause)*
- Become more aware of your feet and your physical body.
- Let us take a moment to thank our Spirit Guides, Angels and loved ones in Spirit for their presence, protection and wisdom whilst we've been working. Knowing that they will always be on hand should we need to call on them. *(Pause)*
- **Now bring your awareness back to your physical body, the chair you are sitting on and your contact with the floor.**
- **Begin to bring some movement back in to your fingers and toes.**
- **In your own time opening your eyes, fully awake and aware and in the physical world.**

(Watch for them starting to wriggle fingers and toes and keep an eye on anyone who doesn't do this. If a member of the group appears not to want to come back to the room simply repeat the last three points, in bold, but raising your voice so that it said slightly louder and firmer. Repeat a third time if necessary moving over to the person and at the end just saying their name and asking that they come back into the room now, placing a hand gently on their shoulder.)

Check to ensure that everyone feels grounded before you finish the session. If not, get them to walk around for a little while. Stamping your feet or jumping up and down helps to bring you back to the physical world. If these don't do the trick, you can ground your energy very readily by eating a small amount of food such as a biscuit.

AND ANOTHER THING:

- Practise dowsing at home by shuffling a pack of cards and placing them face down in a pile. One at a time take the top card and place it in front to you without looking at it. Dowse over it for the information below, write down your result and then put it to one side. Pile the used cards up in the same order so that you can check your answers at the end.
- The first time you try this go through the pack asking for the colour red.
- The second time try to establish each card's suit by asking in turn 'Is it a club?', 'Is it a diamond?', 'Is it a heart?', 'Is it a spade?', until you get a positive reaction.
- The third time try to find all of the picture cards.
- You may also want to try to discover the numbers on the cards, although this will take a bit longer and is more complex. You will probably develop your own system for doing this but you may want to ask question like, Is it a picture card?', 'Is it higher than a 5?' and so on.

Next Time...
The next lesson will be covering CARD READINGS.
You will need to arrange for the following tools to be brought along:
- Your own set of tarot or similar cards

LESSON EIGHT
CARD READINGS

PREPARATION
Well in advance of your meeting ensure that you have all of the tools that you require for this lesson. If not, find out if another group member has access to what you need.

Regular tools:
- Healing book
- Pens and pencils
- Paper
- Candles & matches if desired
- Box of tissues

Tools for this lesson:
- One or more sets of divination or Tarot cards – most people will probably bring their own if they have them, otherwise check that people don't mind sharing theirs with other members of the group.
- Photocopy the required number of the following handouts:
    - '3 Card Spread' – Handout 9 - enough for one per person

On the day of the meeting ensure that the room is prepared:
Are there enough seats for everyone and enough room for the work you are about to undertake?
Open the windows or burn some incense to freshen the air.
Gather the required tools together. Call and remind anyone who has promised to bring something.
Set out some water and glasses. Prepare some relaxing background music.

At the beginning of the meeting:
As people arrive ask them to add the names of anyone they know who needs some healing to the Healing Book. Remember that you don't need to put their full names and private information, first names, initials or nicknames will suffice. Whoever you intend to send the healing to, it will reach.

Once everyone has arrived and is comfortable then you can start.
Work your way through the script and exercises for this lesson as detailed on the following pages.

OPENING & PROTECTION
Read the following script out loud to the group. It's a time of meditation so keep your voice calm and relaxed, reading in a fairly slow and controlled manner. Instructions are in brackets and italics. (Alternatively use the audio CD.)

- Let us take a moment to close our eyes and calm our minds.
- Concentrate on your breathing, allowing the breath to become deeper and slower.

(Pause to allow everyone to take a couple of breaths in and out)

- Let us all mentally ask our Spirit Guides and Angels to draw close and create a circle around our own.
- We let it be known that we are happy to work with Spirit and that we only work in love and light. We ask that anyone from the spirit world who wishes to contact us only does so in love and light and with the highest intentions.

- We ask for your protection, guidance and wisdom as we blend our world with yours. *(Pause)*
- Let us blend and harmonise our energies as we sit together in circle.
- Let us send out a note of harmony to the person on our left. Visualise this as a pale pink mist coming from your heart area and moving towards the heart of the person sitting on your left. *(Pause)*
- As you continue to do this, become aware of receiving the same loving energy from the right.
- As we send and receive this energy, be aware of any changes in the atmosphere within the circle. *(Pause)*
- Have a sense of oneness with the group. *(Pause)*
- Now bring your attention back to yourself and the centre of your being, the lower abdominal area.
- Focus on your breathing; become aware of the rise and fall of your abdomen. As you inhale it will gently rise and as you exhale it will fall. *(Pause to allow everyone to take a few breaths in and out)*
- Have a sense of warmth here and in your mind's eye allow a symbol or shape to form. Imagine that this symbol or shape is sitting at and represents your centre. It may be a simple glow of light, a flame or a flower.
- With each in-breath visualise your symbol becoming larger, stronger or more open whichever is appropriate.
- With each out-breath, imagine that you are exhaling any negativity left from your day, or worries that you may have. *(Pause to allow everyone to take a few breaths in and out)*
- Now take your awareness to the soles of your feet, feeling their contact with the floor. Visualise lines of energy extending out from your feet and down into the ground. In your mind's eye, see these lines of energy as roots extending deep into the earth.
- Earth energy also travels back up through these roots revitalising and nourishing you.
- See this energy entering through the soles of your feet and travelling up through your legs to the base of your spine.
- At the base of the spine imagine that the energy becomes a sphere of deep red mist or light, as you visualise it, it becomes more vibrant in colour. *(Pause)*
- From this point a beam of energy leaves the red sphere and travels up towards the sacral area, just below the belly button. Here it forms a sphere of vibrant orange mist or light. As you focus on it, it becomes stronger in colour. *(Pause)*
- Gradually a beam of energy leaves the orange sphere and travels up towards the solar plexus, where it forms a sphere of clear yellow. With each breath, this yellow becomes stronger and brighter. *(Pause)*
- Once more a beam of energy leaves this sphere and continues its journey up to the heart area. Here a sphere of mist or light begins to form, which you may see as either green or pink. Focus on this area for a few breaths allowing the energy to grow stronger and clearer and to expand. *(Pause)*
- Gradually a beam of energy leaves the heart area and moves upwards to the throat. Here it forms a sphere of clear blue. Once more, as you focus on this area, allow the colour to expand and increase in strength. *(Pause)*
- Now, visualise a strand of energy leaving the throat area and linking with the third eye area, just between and slightly above the eyes. Here energy will begin to form as before. You may see this energy as either a rich indigo or violet, whichever you prefer. Concentrate on this energy and visualise it increasing in strength. *(Pause)*
- Again, a beam of light extends upwards from this area moving to the crown. As it does so, become aware of another beam of energy coming down from above to meet the first. As they meet at the crown a sphere of pure energy begins to form. You may see this energy as either violet or pure white light. This connects you with the higher realms of Spirit.
- As you hold this vision for a few breaths the light grows and strengthens. And as it does so, the beautiful pure light begins to overflow down and around you, surrounding you in its wonderful energy. It fills your aura, cleansing, balancing and strengthening it. You feel safe and comfortable. You feel relaxed and light. *(Longer pause before moving on to the Healing script below.)*

LESSON EIGHT - CARD READINGS

HEALING
- Slowly open your eyes and join hands with those sitting to either side of you. This increases the flow of healing energy.
- We know that our Guides, Angels and loved ones in Spirit have come forward and that they surround us with their healing energies. We ask them to help us as we send out our healing today. *(Pause)*
- Visualise a pool of brilliant white light forming and growing in the middle of our circle. *(Pause)*
- This is a pool of healing energy from which we can all draw when we need to. Know that this universal healing energy will find its way to all of those for whom we request healing.
- We ask for healing for each of us here, for our minds, bodies and spirit.

(If there are absent members: We ask for healing for the members of our group who cannot be with us today.)

- We ask for healing for all of those on our Absent Healing List. Take a moment to visualise them standing the healing pool.
- I would also like to ask for special healing for _____

(Mention anyone else that you feel healing is really important for today. Gently squeeze the hand of the person to your left to indicate that it's their turn. Let everyone have a turn at saying this part before continuing with the script.)

- We send our healing thoughts to Mother Earth and to the plant and animal kingdom. Thank you.
- Release your hands but keep your eyes closed so that you remain relaxed and peaceful as we go in to our meditation. *(Brief pause before moving on to the Meditation script.)*

MEDITATION
- Ensure that you're sitting comfortably with your hands on your knees, palms facing upwards.
- Close your eyes.
- Take a deep inhalation, and breathe out slowly. Continue to breathe slowly and deeply.
- During this meditation you will always be safe and protected, you will feel relaxed and comfortable. If, however, there is anything that does make you feel uneasy, or you wish to come back out of the meditation, you can do so at any time by counting backwards from 3 to 1 and taking a deep breath in and out. You can then bring your awareness back to the physical body, particularly your feet and open your eyes.
- For now though, continue to breathe slowly and deeply, your body feels relaxed and your mind is clear.
- As you breathe images may begin to form in your mind's eye. Don't try to manipulate or analyse them, simply observe them. If you do not automatically see these images, simply imagine or sense them.
- Ahead of you lies a staircase or series of ten steps. Move towards them. At the bottom you can see a doorway. We're going to slowly go down these steps towards the door feeling safe and confident at all times. So moving down the steps on my count:
- 10, 9, 8, with each step feeling lighter and lighter.
- 7, 6, 5, feeling calm and peaceful,
- 4, 3, relaxed and light
- 2 and 1, you find yourself standing in front of the door. Reaching out you open the door and as you do so, a wonderful, warm light shines through from the other side, bathing your whole being in its rays.
- As you stand in this light for a few moments, your physical body is warmed through and your energy body is nourished and energised. This gives you a sense of comfort and completeness and offers further protection on your journey. *(Pause for a short while)*
- Today's journey is designed to help you to connect with the energy of Water. Different watery symbols and representations are common when reading for others and working psychically. Understanding their energy and interpretation can really help you to communicate the correct message to others. Water is particularly linked to the feminine aspect of nature and to our emotions.
- The rays of light subside and you can now see through the doorway to the other side.

- You step through the doorway now and make your way through your sanctuary to the exit that leads to your garden or outside space. Or your sanctuary may already be outside.
- You find yourself on a path that leads you through your beautiful garden or outside space. Follow this path and enjoy the scenery as you walk. Wonderful plants and trees surround you. Notice the colours and the scents. Finally you reach a gateway, beyond is a beautiful wooded area. You go through the gate and follow the path as it winds its way through the woodland alongside a babbling brook. You will have some time to explore this area. The path follows this waterway as it transforms along it's journey to the sea. You may find yourself alongside rivers, lake and waterfalls. You may also encounter creatures from other realms such as water nymphs and mer-people who will guide you on your journey of discovery. If you feel like it, you may drink from the water, wade in it or even swim, it's entirely up to you. Enjoy your time here, connect with the energy of water, its colour, its sound, its feeling, and I will return for you shortly. *(Pause for 5 minutes)*
- It is now time to head back to your sanctuary. So, feeling energised and refreshed, you make your way back along the path that you followed before. Along your way you will find an object lying on the ground. This object is connected with the element of water and has been placed here, just for you. Pick it up, observing it's shape and colour, and hold it as you return along the cliff path to the gateway that leads to your garden.
- Go through the gateway and follow the path through your garden to your sanctuary. Enter your sanctuary and find a safe place such as a windowsill where you can leave your beautiful gift so that you see it whenever you wish to return here. If you have received other gifts during past meditations, you may wish to keep them all together in the same place in your sanctuary.
- Open the door that leads to the stairwell. Step through closing the door behind you.
- Know that your sanctuary is your own space that you can return to at any time for relaxation, guidance and healing.
- And keeping that sense of calm and wellbeing, it is time to head back up the stairs. So moving back up the stairs on my count,
- 1, 2, 3, breathing slowly and deeply,
- 4, 5, 6, your body is starting to feel heavier
- 7, 8, bringing your awareness back to your physical body,
- 9 and 10, on that top step now and when you're ready, step off the top step.
- **Bringing your awareness completely back to your physical body and this room, your contact with the chair, your feet with the floor. Slowly begin to move your fingers and toes, and in your own time, opening your eyes, fully awake and aware and in the physical world.**

(Watch for them starting to wriggle fingers and toes and keep an eye on anyone who doesn't do this. If a member of the group appears not to want to come back to the room simply repeat the last paragraph, in bold, but raising your voice so that it said slightly louder and firmer. Repeat a third time if necessary moving over to the person and at the end just saying their name and asking that they come back now in to the room, placing your hand gently on their shoulder.)

Spend a few minutes sharing experiences of the meditation. Remember that it's okay if someone fell asleep, could see nothing or did their own thing. If you're keeping a personal journal, you may wish to take some time to record you experience. Don't forget to date the entry.

LESSON EIGHT - CARD READINGS

THEORY: CARD READINGS
The following 'theory' section should be read aloud to the group. You may want to get others to join in and take it in turns to read.

We can use 'Tarot' or similar 'Oracle' cards to give readings, to develop our intuition and psychic ability or to inspire and focus our mind with regard to a particular project, event or simply for the day ahead. There are hundreds of different sets of cards available ranging from traditional Tarot decks to cards depicting angels, fairies and mythical creatures. The trick is to find a set which resonates with you and that you feel comfortable using. It's best if you can actually see and handle an open pack or at least view a printout of the images on the cards before selecting a pack to work with. It's preferable not to buy a used or open pack however, as they will be carry some residual energy of whoever has handled the cards. It's quite common for people who read cards to own a number of different packs, although they tend to have a favourite set at any given time. However, if you're just starting out with reading cards, sticking to one pack until you feel more accomplished is probably best.

Some people learn the specific meanings of each card, especially if they are drawn to traditional Tarot. Although this does give a good basis from which to work it's not entirely essential. This is because the cards are simply a tool of divination like any other and form something on which to focus during a reading. If you wish to attend a course dedicated to Tarot reading or teach yourself from a book then that's great. However, there are other ways to develop your skills and to begin to provide insightful and accurate readings for others.

You will develop a way of working or a ritual-like process which states your intention to do a reading and attunes you to the energy of the enquirer. Many readers ask the enquirer to shuffle the cards while thinking of a question or the subject that they want to know about. Then you can ask them to cut the pack if you wish before you deal them out in your chosen spread or pattern so that it's the correct way up for you to read. It's up to you whether you deal them out face down and turn them over and read them one at a time or deal them out face up so that you can immediately start to see a pattern or story unfold. We prefer the latter.

There are a number of different spreads that you can use when giving readings. To begin with the simplest one is to lay down three cards that represent (from left to right):
1) the past or events/people that have led to
2) the present or the current situation or question
3) the future or the potential solution or outcome

As you practise you will intuitively know how the card relates to the enquirer's question. The same card can have entirely different meanings for different people depending on the question being asked, the enquirer's situation, the card's position in the spread, or the information that Spirit wish to convey at that time. When reading the cards, look for a pattern or story in the spread. When you look at them you may be aware of the colours and patterns in the design of the cards or a story that seems to weave its way through the cards. For example, greens and browns can relate to nature and earthly or material matters. Lilacs and purples are more spiritual or psychic colours. The more knowledge you have about different aspects of symbolism and spiritual practise, the more you can analyse the information that you are given. Be aware of things that leap out at you from the cards, or that appear to be brighter or more obvious than usual. What do they symbolise? Animal symbolism may also be appropriate to look into, as can numerology and astrological symbols and associations. This may sound daunting, but take it easy and build up your knowledge slowly and you will be surprised at how your abilities will develop. Remember that this is just the start of your development journey and you are not expected to know everything immediately.

Breathe, relax, clear your mind and then look at and into the cards. Take your time and don't worry about leaving a gap of silence for a little while as you take your time to absorb the information in front of you. Say what you see and what you feel, no matter how silly it may seem. It could be entirely relevant to the enquirer. Words or pictures will start to pop into your head as you become more experienced and it will not be all about what is obviously on the card in front of you.

....

HELEN & DIANE'S TIPS:
- Do what feels comfortable to you: Use the cards and spreads that you like and if you really feel that you don't want to read any particular spread, on a particular occasion or for a particular person, don't do it.
- Whilst some books give specific meaning to inverse (upside down) cards, we never read them as negative. If they arrive in the spread upside down we simply make a mental note of it and turn them up the correct way. It's possible that it can indicate unfulfilled potential.
- Don't panic about getting the DEATH or DEVIL card. They don't foretell death or the presence of evil, but instead indicate (amongst other things) the end of a cycle or the presence of temptation respectively. More can be found on these in a good Tarot book.
- Practise, practise, practise! You may only get a few words for each card to begin with, this is fine, you'll soon become more confident, and as a result you'll get and give more information.
- At first you may wish to use a reference book as a crutch. However, we would recommend putting the book away and using your developing skills of insight and intuition. This may seem hard at first but again, with practise it will soon start to flow.
- Don't be tempted to have lots of card readings yourself, they're there merely as a guide and you shouldn't be running your life by them, and certainly not by the guidance of another person. Additionally, be wary of people becoming over dependant on you giving them readings.
- If, when giving a reading, there feels as though there is a gap between two card explanations, like something is missing or needs clarifying, feel free to pull another card. Simply use the next card in the pack, or shuffle and deal another asking for clarification. Place the card between but slightly above or overlapping the two cards concerned and this should help you read the spread more clearly. You can also do this if you have a real block and can't read the cards on the table. However, don't rely on this method
- In our opinion, no events are cast in stone. They're subject to our free will and we can change future events by decisions or changes that we make in every moment that leads up to them.
- Providing these sorts of readings for others comes with a lot of responsibility. Do not scare or worry enquirer's with negative predictions. Be careful with your wording and treat them gently.

....

PRACTICAL WORK
Read out each exercise, one at a time to the group so that you are all clear as to what you are doing, then allocate a time to complete the exercise.

EXERCISE 1: Singles
- Working in pairs, take it in turns to read for each other.
- Shuffle the pack of cards and fan them out in front of you, face downwards.
- Ask your partner to take one card, as they do so either mentally asking a question, focussing on a situation for which they would like guidance, or asking for a card for the week ahead.
- Practise reading the card for your friend, using the tips and guidelines given in the theory section.

EXERCISE 2: 3-Card Spread
- Working in pairs, take it in turns to read for each other.
- Ask your partner to shuffle the pack of cards, as they do so either mentally asking a question or focussing on a situation for which they would like guidance.

LESSON EIGHT - CARD READINGS

- While they are doing this, prepare by slowing your breathing, relaxing and clearing your mind.
- Take the cards and deal three out in a row in front of you from left to right.
- You can use the 3-card spread (Handout 9) as a guide. The positions relate to:
  1) the past or events/people that have led to
  2) the present or the current situation or question
  3) the future or the potential solution or outcome
- Practise reading the spread, using the tips and guidelines given in the theory section They may want to make notes.
- When you feel that you're finished, discuss your reading and ask them to take a look at the cards. Ask them what they see in them and how they would interpret them. Also discuss how what you've both said relates to their question or situation so that you get feedback from them.

EXERCISE 3: Working Together
- Work in groups of three or four.
- Use the 3 card spread as before and take it in turns to be read by the others in your group.
- For each spread, all look at the cards and say what you see, chip in when you can. You will find that you will feed off of each other's energy in this way.

Leave some time for discussion on how you got on. You may wish to record your findings and readings in a notebook or journal and refer back to them at a later stage.

CLOSING & GROUNDING
Once you have completed the exercises and had some discussion time, everyone should sit comfortably and complete the following meditation to close and ground their energy. Read aloud the following: (or use the audio CD.)

- Sit in a comfortable position and close your eyes.
- Bring your attention to your breathing and focus on this for a few breaths. *(Pause)*
- Take your awareness to the invisible energy field surrounding you and visualise it drawing in close around your physical body. *(Pause)*
- Take your awareness to the area just above your crown and see a sphere of light sitting here.
- Imagine that sphere of light shrinking in size until it's tiny, then sinking down through the crown of your head.
- See it slowly descending down past the brow. *(Pause)*
- Into the throat. *(Pause)*
- Then following the line of the spine, down, through your body, towards your heart area. (Pause)
- Down to your solar plexus. *(Pause)*
- Through the abdominal area. *(Pause)*
- To the base of your spine. *(Pause)*
- Now visualise the sphere of energy either leaving through the base of your spine, or dividing in two and sinking down through your legs and leaving through the soles of your feet.
- Feel this energy leaving you and connecting with the earth.
- Have a sense of downward movement, deep in to the earth. *(Pause)*
- Become more aware of your feet and your physical body.
- Let us take a moment to thank our Spirit Guides, Angels and loved ones in Spirit for their presence, protection and wisdom whilst we've been working. Knowing that they will always be on hand should we need to call on them. *(Pause)*
- **Now bring your awareness back to your physical body, the chair you are sitting on and your contact with the floor.**

- **Begin to bring some movement back in to your fingers and toes.**
- **In your own time opening your eyes, fully awake and aware and in the physical world.**

(Watch for them starting to wriggle fingers and toes and keep an eye on anyone who doesn't do this. If a member of the group appears not to want to come back to the room simply repeat the last three points, in bold, but raising your voice so that it said slightly louder and firmer. Repeat a third time if necessary moving over to the person and at the end just saying their name and asking that they come back into the room now, placing a hand gently on their shoulder.)

Check to ensure that everyone feels grounded before you finish the session. If not, get them to walk around for a little while. Stamping your feet or jumping up and down helps to bring you back to the physical world. If these don't do the trick, you can ground your energy very readily by eating a small amount of food such as a biscuit.

AND ANOTHER THING:
- Read up on symbolism relating to a subject that you enjoy e.g. animal symbols or colours.
- Practise on a friend or by doing readings for a pretend enquirer – lay the cards out – what would you say? What do you see?
- Why not pick a 'card for the day' each morning for a week and see what it says to you? Keep a record of what you 'see' in the card and how it relates to the things that happen to you. If you feel that this is too frequent, what about a 'card for the week'?
- You could pick 12 cards to represent the next 12 months for yourself or a friend. Look for themes for the next year as well as for each individual month. Keep notes to refer back to as the year progresses and see if there are any correspondences.

Next Time...
The next lesson will be covering the subject of ESP / TELEPATHY.
You will need to arrange for the following tools to be brought along:
- Enough sets of Zener cards for one between two group members. One set consists of 5 cards each of the 5 shapes – either photocopy the shapes in the handout section of this book (Appendix Handout 10) on to thin card and cut out to create a pack, or draw the shapes on to uniform pieces of card from a stationers using a black felt pen.
- Each person should also bring a set of five pictures along a theme, such as different pictures of different animals, famous people or nature images (tree, waterfall, fire etc.) in an envelope that they do not show anyone else.
- Take a look at the next lesson and prepare what you need in advance. You may wish to photocopy and hand out the page of symbols so that those who wish to can make their own sets of cards.

LESSON NINE
ESP / TELEPATHY

PREPARATION
Well in advance of your meeting ensure that you have all of the tools that you require for this lesson. If not, find out if another group member has access to what you need.

Regular tools:
- Healing book
- Pens and pencils
- Paper
- Candles & matches if desired
- Box of tissues

Tools for this lesson:
- Enough sets of Zener cards for one between two group members. One set consists of 5 cards each of the 5 shapes – either photocopy the shapes in the handout section of this book (Appendix Handout 10) on to thin card and cut out to create a pack, or draw the shapes on to uniform pieces of card from a stationers using a black felt pen.
- Each person should also bring a set of five pictures along a theme, such as different pictures of different animals, famous people or nature images (tree, waterfall, fire etc.) in an envelope that they do not show anyone else.
- Photocopy the required number of the following handouts:
    - 'ESP Results Record Page' – Handout 11 - enough for 4 per person

On the day of the meeting ensure that the room is prepared:
Are there enough seats for everyone and enough room for the work you are about to undertake?
Open the windows or burn some incense to freshen the air.
Gather the required tools together. Call and remind anyone who has promised to bring something.
Set out some water and glasses.
Prepare some relaxing background music.

At the beginning of the meeting:
As people arrive ask them to add the names of anyone they know who needs some healing to the Healing Book. Remember that you don't need to put their full names and private information, first names, initials or nicknames will suffice. Whoever you intend to send the healing to, it will reach.

Once everyone has arrived and is comfortable then you can start.
Work your way through the script and exercises for this lesson as detailed on the following pages.

OPENING & PROTECTION
Read the following script out loud to the group. It's a time of meditation so keep your voice calm and relaxed, reading in a fairly slow and controlled manner. Instructions are in brackets and italics. (Alternatively use the audio CD.)

○ Let us take a moment to close our eyes and calm our minds.

- Concentrate on your breathing, allowing the breath to become deeper and slower.
  (Pause to allow everyone to take a couple of breaths in and out)
- Let us all mentally ask our Spirit Guides and Angels to draw close and create a circle around our own.
- We let it be known that we are happy to work with Spirit and that we only work in love and light. We ask that anyone from the spirit world who wishes to contact us only does so in love and light and with the highest intentions.
- We ask for your protection, guidance and wisdom as we blend our world with yours. *(Pause)*
- Let us blend and harmonise our energies as we sit together in circle.
- Let us send out a note of harmony to the person on our left. Visualise this as a pale pink mist coming from your heart area and moving towards the heart of the person sitting on your left. *(Pause)*
- As you continue to do this, become aware of receiving the same loving energy from the right.
- As we send and receive this energy, be aware of any changes in the atmosphere within the circle. *(Pause)*
- Have a sense of oneness with the group. *(Pause)*
- Now bring your attention back to yourself and the centre of your being, the lower abdominal area.
- Focus on your breathing; become aware of the rise and fall of your abdomen. As you inhale it will gently rise and as you exhale it will fall. *(Pause to allow everyone to take a few breaths in and out)*
- Have a sense of warmth here and in your mind's eye allow a symbol or shape to form. Imagine that this symbol or shape is sitting at and represents your centre. It may be a simple glow of light, a flame or a flower.
- With each in-breath visualise your symbol becoming larger, stronger or more open whichever is appropriate.
- With each out-breath, imagine that you are exhaling any negativity left from your day, or worries that you may have. *(Pause to allow everyone to take a few breaths in and out)*
- Now take your awareness to the soles of your feet, feeling their contact with the floor. Visualise lines of energy extending out from your feet and down into the ground. In your mind's eye, see these lines of energy as roots extending deep into the earth.
- Earth energy also travels back up through these roots revitalising and nourishing you.
- See this energy entering through the soles of your feet and travelling up through your legs to the base of your spine.
- At the base of the spine imagine that the energy becomes a sphere of deep red mist or light, as you visualise it, it becomes more vibrant in colour. *(Pause)*
- From this point a beam of energy leaves the red sphere and travels up towards the sacral area, just below the belly button. Here it forms a sphere of vibrant orange mist or light. As you focus on it, it becomes stronger in colour. *(Pause)*
- Gradually a beam of energy leaves the orange sphere and travels up towards the solar plexus, where it forms a sphere of clear yellow. With each breath, this yellow becomes stronger and brighter. *(Pause)*
- Once more a beam of energy leaves this sphere and continues its journey up to the heart area. Here a sphere of mist or light begins to form, which you may see as either green or pink. Focus on this area for a few breaths allowing the energy to grow stronger and clearer and to expand. *(Pause)*
- Gradually a beam of energy leaves the heart area and moves upwards to the throat. Here it forms a sphere of clear blue. Once more, as you focus on this area, allow the colour to expand and increase in strength. *(Pause)*
- Now, visualise a strand of energy leaving the throat area and linking with the third eye area, just between and slightly above the eyes. Here energy will begin to form as before. You may see this energy as either a rich indigo or violet, whichever you prefer. Concentrate on this energy and visualise it increasing in strength. *(Pause)*
- Again, a beam of light extends upwards from this area moving to the crown. As it does so, become aware of another beam of energy coming down from above to meet the first. As they meet at the crown a sphere of pure energy begins to form. You may see this energy as either violet or pure

LESSON NINE - ESP / TELEPATHY

white light. This connects you with the higher realms of Spirit.
- As you hold this vision for a few breaths the light grows and strengthens. And as it does so, the beautiful pure light begins to overflow down and around you, surrounding you in its wonderful energy. It fills your aura, cleansing, balancing and strengthening it. You feel safe and comfortable. You feel relaxed and light. *(Longer pause before moving on to the Healing script below.)*

HEALING
- Slowly open your eyes and join hands with those sitting to either side of you. This increases the flow of healing energy.
- We know that our Guides, Angels and loved ones in Spirit have come forward and that they surround us with their healing energies. We ask them to help us as we send out our healing today. *(Pause)*
- Visualise a pool of brilliant white light forming and growing in the middle of our circle. *(Pause)*
- This is a pool of healing energy from which we can all draw when we need to. Know that this universal healing energy will find its way to all of those for whom we request healing.
- We ask for healing for each of us here, for our minds, bodies and spirit.

(If there are absent members: We ask for healing for the members of our group who cannot be with us today.)
- We ask for healing for all of those on our Absent Healing List. Take a moment to visualise them standing the healing pool.
- I would also like to ask for special healing for _____

(Mention anyone else that you feel healing is really important for today. Gently squeeze the hand of the person to your left to indicate that it's their turn. Let everyone have a turn at saying this part before continuing with the script.)
- We send our healing thoughts to Mother Earth and to the plant and animal kingdom. Thank you.
- Release your hands but keep your eyes closed so that you remain relaxed and peaceful as we go in to our meditation. *(Brief pause before moving on to the Meditation script.)*

MEDITATION
- Ensure that you're sitting comfortably with your hands on your knees, palms facing upwards.
- Close your eyes.
- Take a deep inhalation, and breathe out slowly. Continue to breathe slowly and deeply.
- During this meditation you will always be safe and protected, you will feel relaxed and comfortable. If, however, there is anything that does make you feel uneasy, or you wish to come back out of the meditation, you can do so at any time by counting backwards from 3 to 1 and taking a deep breath in and out. You can then bring your awareness back to the physical body, particularly your feet and open your eyes.
- For now though, continue to breathe slowly and deeply, your body feels relaxed and your mind is clear.
- As you breathe images may begin to form in your mind's eye. Don't try to manipulate or analyse them, simply observe them. If you do not automatically see these images, simply imagine or sense them.
- Ahead of you lies a staircase or series of ten steps. Move towards them. At the bottom you can see a doorway. We're going to slowly go down these steps towards the door feeling safe and confident at all times. So moving down the steps on my count:
- 10, 9, 8, with each step feeling lighter and lighter.
- 7, 6, 5, feeling calm and peaceful,
- 4, 3, relaxed and light
- 2 and 1, you find yourself standing in front of the door. Reaching out you open the door and as you do so, a wonderful, warm light shines through from the other side, bathing your whole being in its rays.
- As you stand in this light for a few moments, your physical body is warmed through and your energy body is nourished and energised. This gives you a sense of comfort and completeness and offers further protection on your journey. *(Pause for a short while)*

- Today's journey is designed to help you to connect with your brow, or third eye chakra. This chakra is the one we work with the most when using our Extra-Sensory-Perception.
- The rays of light subside and you can now see through the doorway to the other side.
- As your eyes adjust to the change in light, colours begin to form shapes and you see your sanctuary ahead of you.
- Step through the doorway now and find a comfortable place to sit. Ask your Spirit Guides to draw close to you and help you in developing your awareness.
- As you sit, safe and comfortable in your sanctuary, close your eyes and take your awareness to your brow, or third eye area, just above and between your eyes. Become aware of a sensation here. In your mind's eye, see a small orb of indigo or violet light begin to form at this point. With each breath see it becoming stronger and more vibrant in colour.
- Visualise this orb getting larger and then beginning to extend out in front of you as a tunnel through time and space. As you observe this tunnel there are colours and shapes moving and forming within it. It's not uncomfortable and you remain completely in control and safe.
- You may wish to simply experience these visual sensations and observe the colours and symbols that appear or you may wish to venture into the tunnel with your mind and see what there is to be seen. It's entirely up to you. Whatever you choose, it's safe and comfortable. You are merely observing from a distance. Take some time now to do whatever you prefer and I will return for you shortly. *(Pause for 3-4 minutes)*
- It will soon be time to leave you sanctuary. So bring your awareness back to where you are sitting in your sanctuary, surrounded by your Spirit Guides. Thank them for their protection and assistance with your work. Visualise the brow chakra shrinking back into a smaller orb now. When you feel ready, make your way towards the doorway to the stairwell.
- Open the door that leads to the stairwell. Step through closing the door behind you.
- Know that your sanctuary is your own space that you can return to at any time for relaxation, guidance and healing.
- And keeping that sense of calm and wellbeing, it is time to head back up the stairs. So moving back up the stairs on my count,
- 1, 2, 3, breathing slowly and deeply,
- 4, 5, 6, your body is starting to feel heavier
- 7, 8, bringing your awareness back to your physical body,
- 9 and 10, on that top step now and when you're ready, step off the top step.
- **Bringing your awareness completely back to your physical body and this room, your contact with the chair, your feet with the floor. Slowly begin to move your fingers and toes, and in your own time, opening your eyes, fully awake and aware and in the physical world.**

(Watch for them starting to wriggle fingers and toes and keep an eye on anyone who doesn't do this. If a member of the group appears not to want to come back to the room simply repeat the last paragraph, in bold, but raising your voice so that it said slightly louder and firmer. Repeat a third time if necessary moving over to the person and at the end just saying their name and asking that they come back now in to the room, placing your hand gently on their shoulder.)

Spend a few minutes sharing experiences of the meditation. Remember that it's okay if someone fell asleep, could see nothing or did their own thing. If you're keeping a personal journal, you may wish to take some time to record you experience. Don't forget to date the entry.

NOTE: You may find that this meditation gives you an increased sensitivity or a slight headache at the brow. If this is the case, ask one of the group members to give you some healing before continuing. Healing should be given around the head and shoulders but carefully over the forehead and only if it's not uncomfortable.

THEORY: ESP /TELEPATHY

The following 'theory' section should be read aloud to the group. You may want to get others to join in and take it in turns to read.

ESP and telepathy are an extension of our intuition. ESP or 'Extra-Sensory Perception' is a phrase that encompasses various psychic abilities including clairaudience, telepathy and psychokinesis (that's moving stuff with the power of your mind).

Telepathy is the transfer of thoughts, images or feelings between individuals without verbal or other communication. How often have you known who was calling before picking up the phone? When we have a real connection or rapport with someone it's uncanny how frequently you know what the other is thinking or start to talk about the same subject that they're thinking of, or answer their query before they have even mentioned it.

In 1927, J.B. Rhine, who coined the phrase 'ESP', set up a Parapsychology department at Duke University in the USA. His primary aim was to investigate ESP using very strict scientific tests. He had a 'sender' and a 'receiver' in different rooms with no contact allowed between them. He created the famous 'Zener' cards with basic symbols on them (star, circle, cross, square and wavy line) and the 'sender' used them to send a telepathic picture to the 'receiver'. The results were very exciting. Some of the participants scored highly, far higher than would have been expected if random chance were applied. Over the years many further experiments have been done along similar lines and with similar results, pointing to the existence of telepathy.

We all have a basic telepathic ability and may already be using it without realising. For example, many people receive messages which they choose to dismiss, or take heed of – perhaps you would call it gut instinct? If we go along with the theory that the spirit realms communicate via telepathic means, then it's possibly a loved one or Spirit Guide is passing on advice about a dangerous situation or a potentially life changing encounter. If we do all possess an innate telepathic ability practising the following exercises will help to reawaken it, and logically, by improving our telepathic and E.S.P. skills, it becomes easier to communicate with the spirit world.

One common theory on how this all works is that all knowledge is available to everyone in a big 'pool' of information. The skill is in retrieving the correct and necessary information at any given time. This is the same theory as for most of the subjects covered in this workbook.

It's commonly reported by those seeking to develop their psychic abilities that random words or phrases just pop into their heads for no reason and seemingly with no relevance. It's often described as being like a crossed-line on the phone! Our 'receiver' may be slightly out of tune and picking up a signal that is floating nearby and wasn't meant for us at that moment. All the information that we need is out there and available but it's us as receivers that need the development, or fine-tuning.

HELEN & DIANE'S TIPS:
- It's important not to become frustrated when first trying out the telepathic exercises – as we've said many times in this workbook, the key is to keep practising and you'll undoubtedly see your abilities improve. Some of the most talented mediums struggle to get decent results using Zener cards but this is possibly because they feel under pressure to achieve amazing results. This can cause a block in itself.
- The key, as always is to relax, allow the information to flow into your mind and then be confident enough to give that information as your answer.
- You may find that you're more proficient in either sending or receiving. This is quite common. In time you will improve in both areas.
- You may also have different results with different people because you're more naturally 'in tune' with them.
- Don't overdo it, your mind will become tired after a while and this will affect your results. Sometimes we've found that over-practise in any one session can cause a bit of a headache.

PRACTICAL WORK
Read out each exercise, one at a time to the group so that you are all clear as to what you are doing, then allocate a time to complete the exercise.

For our practical work, we are going to concentrate on telepathy.

EXERCISE 1: Zener Cards
- Work in pairs, each pair having their own set of cards.
- One person will be the sender, the other the receiver.
- Read out these instructions to everyone before you start.
- You can sit opposite each other or back to back. You can even try working in different rooms if you wish, although you might want to practise a few times first before trying this.
- Ensure that there are no mirrors or other reflective surfaces around the room before you start.
- For your first attempt you will start by sending five symbols. As you get more experienced you may want to send 10, 15, 20, and eventually 25 in one session.
- Both partners should use their own copy of the ESP Results Record Page. Fill in your names and the date at the top.
- The sender should use it to record which symbols they draw from the cards and 'send' to their partner, in the 'sent' column.
- The receiver should use it to record the symbols that they feel are being sent to them in the 'received' column. As this exercise requires a fair amount of concentration it's better to write the answers down as you go along, rather than saying them aloud and disrupting concentration on both sides.
- The sender shuffles their pack, holding it face down, and then turns the first one over and concentrates on this image. See it being sent into the mind of your partner. You may wish to say '1st card', '2nd card' etc. before sending each one.
- The receiver should write down the first image that comes to mind. Remember to use the first thought before you start to question yourself!
- Repeat until the desired number of cards have been sent and received.
- Compare your results sheets and record the details in the blank 'sent' or 'received' column from your partner's sheet so that you both have a complete record of the exercise. Give yourself a mark out of 5 but do not over analyse the results at this stage.
- Swap over and repeat the exercise the other way around.

LESSON NINE - ESP / TELEPATHY

- If you wish, repeat this exercise with different partners.
- Once you have finished, take a look at your results using Exercise 2.

EXERCISE 2: Analyse
- Discuss your experiences and compare your results.
- Getting the correct results due to chance occur at the rate of 1 in 5 or 20%. Anything more than this is a positive result.
- Equally, anything less than that should be looked at. Is there a pattern? Are you always mistaking the same symbol for a different one? Are you out of step, one behind or even in front?
- It's interesting to analyse your results like this, but also to keep a dated record of them and compare them with future exercise to see how you improve.

These results show that you seem to be out of step, or one behind.

	Symbol sent	Symbol received
1	□	+
2	○	□
3	☆	○
4	≋	☆
5	□	≋

These results show that you seem to be one ahead indicating prescience or foreknowledge.

	Symbol sent	Symbol received
1	□	○
2	○	☆
3	☆	≋
4	≋	□
5	□	☆

These results show that you have 0 out of 5 correct which is less than chance. However, if you look again, there is a consistent error where the square is mistaken for the corss and vice versa. Practise will help you to fine-tune your ability.

	Symbol sent	Symbol received
1	□	+
2	○	≋
3	□	+
4	≋	☆
5	+	□

EXERCISE 3: Images
- Read the following instructions out before you begin.
- Work in pairs again, sitting opposite each other.
- You're going to repeat Exercise 1 but using the images you've brought with you.
- This time you have more information to convey to the receiver, e.g. different colours, shapes and other imagery. See if this makes it easier or more difficult for you when sending and when receiving.
- You may find it easier to break the image down into the different shapes that make up the pictures to begin with. For example, if you have a picture of a sailing boat, you may send or receive the image of a triangle for the sail, to help your partner build up the picture.
- The sender should number their pictures 1 to 5 and say something like, 'I am now sending picture 1' as appropriate, before focussing on that image.
- The receiver should use separate pieces of blank paper this time. Write on it the sender's and receiver's names and the date before you start. Label the first page, 'picture 1' and use the page to record what you get in your mind's eye. You may wish to write down notes, such as details of shapes, colours, emotions etc. that you are getting. Alternatively you may wish to sketch or doodle while you are receiving to see what shapes come through.
- Work through the five pictures and then swap over and repeat. If you feel five is too much just do what you can.
- You may find it useful to set a timer to go off so that you focus on one image for 2 minutes and then move on to the next.

CLOSING & GROUNDING
Once you have completed the exercises and had some discussion time, everyone should sit comfortably and complete the following meditation to close and ground their energy. Read aloud the following: (or use the audio CD.)

- Sit in a comfortable position and close your eyes.
- Bring your attention to your breathing and focus on this for a few breaths. *(Pause)*
- Take your awareness to the invisible energy field surrounding you and visualise it drawing in close around your physical body. *(Pause)*
- Take your awareness to the area just above your crown and see a sphere of light sitting here.
- Imagine that sphere of light shrinking in size until it's tiny, then sinking down through the crown of your head.
- See it slowly descending down past the brow. *(Pause)*
- Into the throat. *(Pause)*
- Then following the line of the spine, down, through your body, towards your heart area. (Pause)
- Down to your solar plexus. *(Pause)*
- Through the abdominal area. *(Pause)*
- To the base of your spine. *(Pause)*
- Now visualise the sphere of energy either leaving through the base of your spine, or dividing in two and sinking down through your legs and leaving through the soles of your feet.
- Feel this energy leaving you and connecting with the earth.
- Have a sense of downward movement, deep in to the earth. *(Pause)*
- Become more aware of your feet and your physical body.
- Let us take a moment to thank our Spirit Guides, Angels and loved ones in Spirit for their presence, protection and wisdom whilst we've been working. Knowing that they will always be on hand should we need to call on them. *(Pause)*
- **Now bring your awareness back to your physical body, the chair you are sitting on and your contact with the floor.**

LESSON NINE - ESP / TELEPATHY

- **Begin to bring some movement back in to your fingers and toes.**
- **In your own time opening your eyes, fully awake and aware and in the physical world.**

(Watch for them starting to wriggle fingers and toes and keep an eye on anyone who doesn't do this. If a member of the group appears not to want to come back to the room simply repeat the last three points, in bold, but raising your voice so that it said slightly louder and firmer. Repeat a third time if necessary moving over to the person and at the end just saying their name and asking that they come back into the room now, placing a hand gently on their shoulder.)

Check to ensure that everyone feels grounded before you finish the session. If not, get them to walk around for a little while. Stamping your feet or jumping up and down helps to bring you back to the physical world. If these don't do the trick, you can ground your energy very readily by eating a small amount of food such as a biscuit.

AND ANOTHER THING:

- Keep practising!
- A good book on this subject that's really easy to use and understand is 'The Telepathy Kit' by Tara Ward.
- Whenever your telephone rings unexpectedly, try to predict who it is before answering it. You may like to keep a note of how accurate you are with this.
- Be more aware of things that happen where you somehow knew about them beforehand – the things that you might have previously put down to coincidence. Keeping a diary or journal, which could include details of your dreams would be a useful record to look back at in the future. You should find that as your overall psychic awareness develops there are more and more of these occasions.

Next Time...
The next lesson will be covering OTHER METHODS OF DIVINATION.
You will need to arrange for the following tools to be brought along:
- Teapot, cups and saucers & some tea leaves
- One or more of the following: crystal ball, obsidian mirror or a bowl of water
- If using a bowl of water you can add oil, dark ink or candle wax to create shapes
- Notebooks and pens.
- Any tools that you haven't yet had a chance to try such as a crystal ball, runes etc. but EXCLUDING a ouija board.

LESSON TEN
OTHER METHODS OF DIVINATION

PREPARATION
Well in advance of your meeting ensure that you have all of the tools that you require for this lesson. If not, find out if another group member has access to what you need.

Regular tools:
- Healing book
- Pens and pencils
- Paper
- Candles & matches if desired
- Box of tissues

Tools for this lesson:
- Members should be bringing along any divination tools that they wish to try out during this lesson, EXCLUDING a ouija board.
- Tea leaves, teapot, cups and saucers.
- One or more of the following: crystal ball, obsidian mirror, bowl of water.
- If using a bowl of water you can add oil, dark ink or candle wax to create shapes.
- Photocopy the required number of the following handouts:
    - 'Psychic Symbols' - Handout 12 - enough for one per person

On the day of the meeting ensure that the room is prepared:
Are there enough seats for everyone and enough room for the work you are about to undertake?
Open the windows or burn some incense to freshen the air.
Gather the required tools together. Call and remind anyone who has promised to bring something.
Set out some water and glasses.
Prepare some relaxing background music.

At the beginning of the meeting:
As people arrive ask them to add the names of anyone they know who needs some healing to the Healing Book. Remember that you don't need to put their full names and private information, first names, initials or nicknames will suffice. Whoever you intend to send the healing to, it will reach.

Once everyone has arrived and is comfortable then you can start.
Work your way through the script and exercises for this lesson as detailed on the following pages.

OPENING & PROTECTION
Read the following script out loud to the group. It's a time of meditation so keep your voice calm and relaxed, reading in a fairly slow and controlled manner. Instructions are in brackets and italics. (Alternatively use the audio CD.)

- Let us take a moment to close our eyes and calm our minds.
- Concentrate on your breathing, allowing the breath to become deeper and slower.

(Pause to allow everyone to take a couple of breaths in and out)

- Let us all mentally ask our Spirit Guides and Angels to draw close and create a circle around our own.
- We let it be known that we are happy to work with Spirit and that we only work in love and light. We ask that anyone from the spirit world who wishes to contact us only does so in love and light and with the highest intentions.
- We ask for your protection, guidance and wisdom as we blend our world with yours. *(Pause)*
- Let us blend and harmonise our energies as we sit together in circle.
- Let us send out a note of harmony to the person on our left. Visualise this as a pale pink mist coming from your heart area and moving towards the heart of the person sitting on your left. *(Pause)*
- As you continue to do this, become aware of receiving the same loving energy from the right.
- As we send and receive this energy, be aware of any changes in the atmosphere within the circle. *(Pause)*
- Have a sense of oneness with the group. *(Pause)*
- Now bring your attention back to yourself and the centre of your being, the lower abdominal area.
- Focus on your breathing; become aware of the rise and fall of your abdomen. As you inhale it will gently rise and as you exhale it will fall. *(Pause to allow everyone to take a few breaths in and out)*
- Have a sense of warmth here and in your mind's eye allow a symbol or shape to form. Imagine that this symbol or shape is sitting at and represents your centre. It may be a simple glow of light, a flame or a flower.
- With each in-breath visualise your symbol becoming larger, stronger or more open whichever is appropriate.
- With each out-breath, imagine that you are exhaling any negativity left from your day, or worries that you may have. *(Pause to allow everyone to take a few breaths in and out)*
- Now take your awareness to the soles of your feet, feeling their contact with the floor. Visualise lines of energy extending out from your feet and down into the ground. In your mind's eye, see these lines of energy as roots extending deep into the earth.
- Earth energy also travels back up through these roots revitalising and nourishing you.
- See this energy entering through the soles of your feet and travelling up through your legs to the base of your spine.
- At the base of the spine imagine that the energy becomes a sphere of deep red mist or light, as you visualise it, it becomes more vibrant in colour. *(Pause)*
- From this point a beam of energy leaves the red sphere and travels up towards the sacral area, just below the belly button. Here it forms a sphere of vibrant orange mist or light. As you focus on it, it becomes stronger in colour. *(Pause)*
- Gradually a beam of energy leaves the orange sphere and travels up towards the solar plexus, where it forms a sphere of clear yellow. With each breath, this yellow becomes stronger and brighter. *(Pause)*
- Once more a beam of energy leaves this sphere and continues its journey up to the heart area. Here a sphere of mist or light begins to form, which you may see as either green or pink. Focus on this area for a few breaths allowing the energy to grow stronger and clearer and to expand. *(Pause)*
- Gradually a beam of energy leaves the heart area and moves upwards to the throat. Here it forms a sphere of clear blue. Once more, as you focus on this area, allow the colour to expand and increase in strength. *(Pause)*
- Now, visualise a strand of energy leaving the throat area and linking with the third eye area, just between and slightly above the eyes. Here energy will begin to form as before. You may see this energy as either a rich indigo or violet, whichever you prefer. Concentrate on this energy and visualise it increasing in strength. *(Pause)*
- Again, a beam of light extends upwards from this area moving to the crown. As it does so, become aware of another beam of energy coming down from above to meet the first. As they meet at the crown a sphere of pure energy begins to form. You may see this energy as either violet or pure white light. This connects you with the higher realms of Spirit.
- As you hold this vision for a few breaths the light grows and strengthens. And as it does so, the beau-

tiful pure light begins to overflow down and around you, surrounding you in its wonderful energy. It fills your aura, cleansing, balancing and strengthening it. You feel safe and comfortable. You feel relaxed and light. *(Longer pause before moving on to the Healing script below.)*

HEALING
- Slowly open your eyes and join hands with those sitting to either side of you. This increases the flow of healing energy.
- We know that our Guides, Angels and loved ones in Spirit have come forward and that they surround us with their healing energies. We ask them to help us as we send out our healing today. *(Pause)*
- Visualise a pool of brilliant white light forming and growing in the middle of our circle. *(Pause)*
- This is a pool of healing energy from which we can all draw when we need to. Know that this universal healing energy will find its way to all of those for whom we request healing.
- We ask for healing for each of us here, for our minds, bodies and spirit.

(If there are absent members: We ask for healing for the members of our group who cannot be with us today.)
- We ask for healing for all of those on our Absent Healing List. Take a moment to visualise them standing the healing pool.
- I would also like to ask for special healing for _____

(Mention anyone else that you feel healing is really important for today. Gently squeeze the hand of the person to your left to indicate that it's their turn. Let everyone have a turn at saying this part before continuing with the script.)
- We send our healing thoughts to Mother Earth and to the plant and animal kingdom. Thank you.
- Release your hands but keep your eyes closed so that you remain relaxed and peaceful as we go in to our meditation. *(Brief pause before moving on to the Meditation script.)*

MEDITATION
- Ensure that you're sitting comfortably with your hands on your knees, palms facing upwards.
- Close your eyes.
- Take a deep inhalation, and breathe out slowly. Continue to breathe slowly and deeply.
- During this meditation you will always be safe and protected, you will feel relaxed and comfortable. If, however, there is anything that does make you feel uneasy, or you wish to come back out of the meditation, you can do so at any time by counting backwards from 3 to 1 and taking a deep breath in and out. You can then bring your awareness back to the physical body, particularly your feet and open your eyes.
- For now though, continue to breathe slowly and deeply, your body feels relaxed and your mind is clear.
- As you breathe images may begin to form in your mind's eye. Don't try to manipulate or analyse them, simply observe them. If you do not automatically see these images, simply imagine or sense them.
- Ahead of you lies a staircase or series of ten steps. Move towards them. At the bottom you can see a doorway. We're going to slowly go down these steps towards the door feeling safe and confident at all times. So moving down the steps on my count:
- 10, 9, 8, with each step feeling lighter and lighter.
- 7, 6, 5, feeling calm and peaceful,
- 4, 3, relaxed and light
- 2 and 1, you find yourself standing in front of the door. Reaching out you open the door and as you do so, a wonderful, warm light shines through from the other side, bathing your whole being in its rays.
- As you stand in this light for a few moments, your physical body is warmed through and your energy body is nourished and energised. This gives you a sense of comfort and completeness and offers further protection on your journey. *(Pause for a short while)*
- Today's journey is designed to help you to awaken your senses and psychic being.

- The rays of light subside and you can now see through the doorway to your sanctuary on the other side.
- You step through and make your way through your sanctuary to the exit that leads to your garden or outside space. Or your sanctuary may be an outside space itself.
- You find yourself on a path that leads you through your beautiful garden or outside space. Follow this path and enjoy the scenery as you walk. You are surrounded by wonderful plants and trees. Notice the colours and the scents. Finally you reach a gateway, which gives you access to a cliff path. The path is wide and safe and you decide to go through the gate and follow it up to the cliffs. You feel safe and secure as you do so. *(Pause)*
- Look around you. What do you see? Perhaps the first thing you will notice is the turquoise blue sea below you, glistening in the warm hazy sunshine. Perhaps your eyes will be drawn to the soft golden sand. Take time to observe everything around you. Your eyes are alert and focussed, and can see far into the distance. Allow yourself some time to simply look and take in everything around you. *(Pause for a minute)*
- Now that your eyes have registered your beautiful surroundings, gently close them and allow your sense of smell to take over. Breathe in the crisp clean air. With each breath that you take, acknowledge the scents that surround you. The aroma of the salty sea brought to you upon the gentle breeze. The scent of the flowers and grass on the cliff top. Breathe in the wonderful smells, allowing them to fill your lungs, cleansing and rejuvenating you. *(Pause for 30 seconds or so).*
- Now take your awareness to your hearing. Allow all other sensations to fade away as you listen to the sounds around you. Hear the gentle lapping of the waves against the rocks below you. Listen to the seagulls calling. Hear the soft breeze blowing through the grass around you. Spend a few moments listening to everything. *(Pause for 30 seconds or so).*
- Now reach out and touch the grass below your feet. Feel its soft texture between your fingers. Move your hands to the flowers around you, feeling the silkiness of their petals. Perhaps there are stones or crystals in the rock faces around you. Touch them, allowing yourself to acknowledge how they feel. *(Pause for 30 seconds or so)*
- Now that you have awakened your senses, find a place on the cliff-top to sit quietly. You feel both centred and peaceful. Spend some time in this wonderful place, seeing, sensing, touching, hearing and smelling all the things around you. All of your senses feel heightened as you relax on your cliff top. Allow yourself to experience anything that you need to experience, feeling safe and secure at all times. I will leave you here for a while and return for you shortly. *(Pause for 2-3 minutes)*
- It's now time to leave your cliff-top. Stand up and begin walking back over the cliff-top, and along the path. As you walk, remain aware of everything around you. Your senses will remain finely tuned as you return to the physical plane.
- Open the door that leads to the stairwell. Step through closing the door behind you.
- Know that your sanctuary is your own space that you can return to at any time for relaxation, guidance and healing.
- And keeping that sense of calm and wellbeing, it is time to head back up the stairs. So moving back up the stairs on my count,
- 1, 2, 3, breathing slowly and deeply,
- 4, 5, 6, your body is starting to feel heavier
- 7, 8, bringing your awareness back to your physical body,
- 9 and 10, on that top step now and when you're ready, step off the top step.
- **Bringing your awareness completely back to your physical body and this room, your contact with the chair, your feet with the floor. Slowly begin to move your fingers and toes, and in your own time, opening your eyes, fully awake and aware and in the physical world.**

(Watch for them starting to wriggle fingers and toes and keep an eye on anyone who doesn't do this. If a member of the group appears not to want to come back to the room simply repeat the last paragraph, in bold, but raising your voice so that it said slightly louder and firmer. Repeat a third time if necessary moving over

to the person and at the end just saying their name and asking that they come back now in to the room, placing your hand gently on their shoulder.)

Spend a few minutes sharing experiences of the meditation. Remember that it's okay if someone fell asleep, could see nothing or did their own thing. If you're keeping a personal journal, you may wish to take some time to record you experience. Don't forget to date the entry.

THEORY: OTHER METHODS OF DIVINATION
The following 'theory' section should be read aloud to the group. You may want to get others to join in and take it in turns to read.

There are many forms of divination some of which we have covered already such as card readings, reading the aura, and dowsing. Other examples are runes, dream analysis, tea leaf reading, crystal readings, and scrying.

There are two exercises given in the practical section of this lesson, one for tea leaf reading and one for scrying.

Scrying can take many forms - the most common of which is crystal ball readings. Other ways include using mirrors, bowls of water, ink or oil dropped in water - in fact anything with a reflective surface. Some people also look for the formation of symbols in clouds, fire or candle flames.

Both methods are yet more building blocks in developing our abilities. They are like many of the other tools and skills that we learn in that they act as a catalyst and a focus for our innate abilities, enabling us to tune in more easily.

We have covered some theory on symbol reading previously. Scrying is similar but may need some further explanation. Scrying comes from the old english word 'descry' meaning "to make out dimly" or "to reveal". So we are asking the tools that we use to reveal messages to us that we can then read and interpret.

Scrying has been used for thousands of years by different cultures. The ancient Egyptians used scrying. One legend states that the goddess Hathor carried a shield that could reflect back all things in their true light. From this shield she allegedly fashioned the first magic mirror to scry with. The ancient Greeks and Celts, Nostradamus and a famous alchemist John Dee are also believed to have used various methods of scrying.

....

HELEN & DIANE'S TIPS:
- Using divination tools requires practise and patience.
- Many people find candlelight very useful when learning to scry as it helps to create shadows and the right ambience.
- Often it's the interpretation of the symbols that takes time to learn rather than the ability to see images in the first place.
- Some people can actually view images upon the reflective surface. Others simply use the shadows and reflected light patterns, which create shapes and reflections.
- Use whichever method works for you and remember to simply give what you feel.
- As with all psychic matters don't allow logic to interrupt, although this is easier said than done!
- Performing a simple relaxation exercise or meditation as part of your preparation will allow you to relax and tune in, giving you a better chance of being successful.
- Remember you may be better at some types of scrying than others.

....

PRACTICAL WORK
Read out each exercise, one at a time to the group so that you are all clear as to what you are doing, then allocate a time to complete the exercise.

Choose from the following exercises. If you have time, have a go at the others.
Give out the 'Psychic Symbols' handouts to help with interpreting the symbols.

EXERCISE 1: Up To You
- Choose a method of divination that you would like to try.
- Either use the tools you've brought along or team up with someone who has brought something that you are drawn to.
- Work in pairs or as a group and all read for one person at a time.
- The buzz that this creates helps you to get more information through as you feed off of each other.

EXERCISE 2: Tea Leaf Reading:
- Work in pairs to do these readings.
- Make a pot of tea, using leaves *not* bags.
- Pour a cup of tea for each person taking part and allow the leaves to settle in the cup.
- Drink the tea leaving a small amount at the bottom of the cup containing the leaves.
- Turn the cup upside down on to the saucer allowing the remaining liquid to run out.
- Turn the cup three times in a clockwise manner on the saucer and pass it to your partner.
- The reader can then turn the cup over and take a look at the leaves.
- The reader should look for patterns and shapes or symbols that have been formed by the leaves. What do these symbols mean to you? What might they relate to? As you begin to interpret them, more thoughts or images may come into your mind. Use the patterns in the cup as a tool or trigger to open you to the messages waiting for the enquirer.
- Keep a record of the reading including the date and names of the enquirer and reader.
- Swap over so that everyone gets a go.

EXERCISE 3: Scrying
- For this exercise there are many things you can use to gaze into: crystal ball, obsidian mirror, bowl of water, a bowl of water with a small amount of oil, dark ink or wax dropped into, even a candle flame, incense smoke or a fire.
- Work in pairs.
- Read through the following instructions before you start. If necessary, one person can talk you through the instructions. Use a room with dimmed lights, light a couple of candles only, placed low and behind you.
- Close your eyes and concentrate on your breathing. Visualise yourself surrounded by white light. Allow yourself to relax and your breathing to slow.
- Focus your intention on reading for your partner.
- When you feel ready, slowly open your eyes and look upon the reflective surface.
- Turn or move the item until you have as few reflections as possible and you cannot see yourself, then allow your eyes to relax and gaze at the object, looking through it not at it.
- You may see a cloudiness forming (especially with the crystal ball). Let it form, then keep watching as it begins to clear.
- It's natural when you first see something to jolt and lose your concentration. Just start again, you will soon get used to it.
- Try not to stare or push things too much - allow things to happen slowly and be prepared to try a few times before you get results.

LESSON TEN - OTHER METHODS OF DIVINATION

- Tell your partner what you are seeing so that they can make a note of it.
- Keep a record of the reading including the date and names of the enquirer and reader.
- Swap over so that you both get a go.

Discuss your experiences with the rest of the group. How did you find it? Which tools did you prefer?

CLOSING & GROUNDING
Once you have completed the exercises and had some discussion time, everyone should sit comfortably and complete the following meditation to close and ground their energy. Read aloud the following: (or use the audio CD.)

- Sit in a comfortable position and close your eyes.
- Bring your attention to your breathing and focus on this for a few breaths. *(Pause)*
- Take your awareness to the invisible energy field surrounding you and visualise it drawing in close around your physical body. *(Pause)*
- Take your awareness to the area just above your crown and see a sphere of light sitting here.
- Imagine that sphere of light shrinking in size until it's tiny, then sinking down through the crown of your head.
- See it slowly descending down past the brow. *(Pause)*
- Into the throat. *(Pause)*
- Then following the line of the spine, down, through your body, towards your heart area. (Pause)
- Down to your solar plexus. *(Pause)*
- Through the abdominal area. *(Pause)*
- To the base of your spine. *(Pause)*
- Now visualise the sphere of energy either leaving through the base of your spine, or dividing in two and sinking down through your legs and leaving through the soles of your feet.
- Feel this energy leaving you and connecting with the earth.
- Have a sense of downward movement, deep in to the earth. *(Pause)*
- Become more aware of your feet and your physical body.
- Let us take a moment to thank our Spirit Guides, Angels and loved ones in Spirit for their presence, protection and wisdom whilst we've been working. Knowing that they will always be on hand should we need to call on them. *(Pause)*
- **Now bring your awareness back to your physical body, the chair you are sitting on and your contact with the floor.**
- **Begin to bring some movement back in to your fingers and toes.**
- **In your own time opening your eyes, fully awake and aware and in the physical world.**

(Watch for them starting to wriggle fingers and toes and keep an eye on anyone who doesn't do this. If a member of the group appears not to want to come back to the room simply repeat the last three points, in bold, but raising your voice so that it said slightly louder and firmer. Repeat a third time if necessary moving over to the person and at the end just saying their name and asking that they come back into the room now, placing a hand gently on their shoulder.)

Check to ensure that everyone feels grounded before you finish the session. If not, get them to walk around for a little while. Stamping your feet or jumping up and down helps to bring you back to the physical world. If these don't do the trick, you can ground your energy very readily by eating a small amount of food such as a biscuit.

AND ANOTHER THING:
- Keep trying new things, until you find something you really click with. Or maybe you've already found it. You can then focus on this method of divination until you feel really comfortable and confident with it.
- There are many other forms of divination, for example cloud scrying, divination using dice or ribbon readings. Take time to research these and find new things to try.
- Remember that scrying and tea leaf reading will be particularly useful to those who are more naturally clairvoyant. If your abilities lie elsewhere you may prefer to concentrate on other things such as telepathy or psychometry until your own clairvoyance is more developed.

Next Time...
The next lesson will be covering the subject of
NATIVE AMERICAN WISDOM & TOTEM ANIMALS.
You will need to arrange for the following tools to be brought along:
- a compass
- four fairly large crystals or stones
- any books that you have on animal symbolism such as 'Animal Speak' by Ted Andrews
- any sets of cards you may have which relate to totem animals such Medicine Cards by Jamie Sams – this set also comes with a book to help translate the messages that each of the animals bring. Or you could start creating your own.

LESSON ELEVEN
NATIVE AMERICAN WISDOM & TOTEM ANIMALS

PREPARATION
Well in advance of your meeting ensure that you have all of the tools that you require for this lesson. If not, find out if another group member has access to what you need.

Regular tools:
- Healing book
- Pens and pencils
- Paper
- Candles & matches if desired
- Box of tissues

Tools for this lesson:
- A set of Animal Divination or Totem cards. If you are unable to obtain a set to use, you may want to make your own.
- Any reference books that members of the group have or can borrow on animal symbolism.
- Take a look at Exercise 2. If you feel that you have the space to do this, you will need:
- 4 large stones or crystal points.
- A compass
- Photocopy the required number of the following handouts:
    - 'Animal Symbolism' - Handout 13 - enough for one per person
    - 'Compass Point Cards' - Handout 14 - enough for one per person + 1 for the medicine wheel

On the day of the meeting ensure that the room is prepared:
Are there enough seats for everyone and enough room for the work you are about to undertake?
Open the windows or burn some incense to freshen the air.
Gather the required tools together. Call and remind anyone who has promised to bring something.
Set out some water and glasses.
Prepare some relaxing background music.

At the beginning of the meeting:
As people arrive ask them to add the names of anyone they know who needs some healing to the Healing Book. Remember that you don't need to put their full names and private information, first names, initials or nicknames will suffice. Whoever you intend to send the healing to, it will reach.

Once everyone has arrived and is comfortable then you can start.
Work your way through the script and exercises for this lesson as detailed on the following pages.

OPENING & PROTECTION
Read the following script out loud to the group. It's a time of meditation so keep your voice calm and relaxed, reading in a fairly slow and controlled manner. Instructions are in brackets and italics. (Alternatively use the audio CD.)

○ Let us take a moment to close our eyes and calm our minds.

THE SPIRITUAL & PSYCHIC WORKBOOK – A COURSE COMPANION

- Concentrate on your breathing, allowing the breath to become deeper and slower.
  (Pause to allow everyone to take a couple of breaths in and out)
- Let us all mentally ask our Spirit Guides and Angels to draw close and create a circle around our own.
- We let it be known that we are happy to work with Spirit and that we only work in love and light. We ask that anyone from the spirit world who wishes to contact us only does so in love and light and with the highest intentions.
- We ask for your protection, guidance and wisdom as we blend our world with yours. *(Pause)*
- Let us blend and harmonise our energies as we sit together in circle.
- Let us send out a note of harmony to the person on our left. Visualise this as a pale pink mist coming from your heart area and moving towards the heart of the person sitting on your left. *(Pause)*
- As you continue to do this, become aware of receiving the same loving energy from the right.
- As we send and receive this energy, be aware of any changes in the atmosphere within the circle. *(Pause)*
- Have a sense of oneness with the group. *(Pause)*
- Now bring your attention back to yourself and the centre of your being, the lower abdominal area.
- Focus on your breathing; become aware of the rise and fall of your abdomen. As you inhale it will gently rise and as you exhale it will fall. *(Pause to allow everyone to take a few breaths in and out)*
- Have a sense of warmth here and in your mind's eye allow a symbol or shape to form. Imagine that this symbol or shape is sitting at and represents your centre. It may be a simple glow of light, a flame or a flower.
- With each in-breath visualise your symbol becoming larger, stronger or more open whichever is appropriate.
- With each out-breath, imagine that you are exhaling any negativity left from your day, or worries that you may have. *(Pause to allow everyone to take a few breaths in and out)*
- Now take your awareness to the soles of your feet, feeling their contact with the floor. Visualise lines of energy extending out from your feet and down into the ground. In your mind's eye, see these lines of energy as roots extending deep into the earth.
- Earth energy also travels back up through these roots revitalising and nourishing you.
- See this energy entering through the soles of your feet and travelling up through your legs to the base of your spine.
- At the base of the spine imagine that the energy becomes a sphere of deep red mist or light, as you visualise it, it becomes more vibrant in colour. *(Pause)*
- From this point a beam of energy leaves the red sphere and travels up towards the sacral area, just below the belly button. Here it forms a sphere of vibrant orange mist or light. As you focus on it, it becomes stronger in colour. *(Pause)*
- Gradually a beam of energy leaves the orange sphere and travels up towards the solar plexus, where it forms a sphere of clear yellow. With each breath, this yellow becomes stronger and brighter. *(Pause)*
- Once more a beam of energy leaves this sphere and continues its journey up to the heart area. Here a sphere of mist or light begins to form, which you may see as either green or pink. Focus on this area for a few breaths allowing the energy to grow stronger and clearer and to expand. *(Pause)*
- Gradually a beam of energy leaves the heart area and moves upwards to the throat. Here it forms a sphere of clear blue. Once more, as you focus on this area, allow the colour to expand and increase in strength. *(Pause)*
- Now, visualise a strand of energy leaving the throat area and linking with the third eye area, just between and slightly above the eyes. Here energy will begin to form as before. You may see this energy as either a rich indigo or violet, whichever you prefer. Concentrate on this energy and visualise it increasing in strength. *(Pause)*
- Again, a beam of light extends upwards from this area moving to the crown. As it does so, become aware of another beam of energy coming down from above to meet the first. As they meet at the crown a sphere of pure energy begins to form. You may see this energy as either violet or pure

white light. This connects you with the higher realms of Spirit.
- As you hold this vision for a few breaths the light grows and strengthens. And as it does so, the beautiful pure light begins to overflow down and around you, surrounding you in its wonderful energy. It fills your aura, cleansing, balancing and strengthening it. You feel safe and comfortable. You feel relaxed and light. *(Longer pause before moving on to the Healing script below.)*

HEALING
- Slowly open your eyes and join hands with those sitting to either side of you. This increases the flow of healing energy.
- We know that our Guides, Angels and loved ones in Spirit have come forward and that they surround us with their healing energies. We ask them to help us as we send out our healing today. *(Pause)*
- Visualise a pool of brilliant white light forming and growing in the middle of our circle. *(Pause)*
- This is a pool of healing energy from which we can all draw when we need to. Know that this universal healing energy will find its way to all of those for whom we request healing.
- We ask for healing for each of us here, for our minds, bodies and spirit.

(If there are absent members: We ask for healing for the members of our group who cannot be with us today.)
- We ask for healing for all of those on our Absent Healing List. Take a moment to visualise them standing the healing pool.
- I would also like to ask for special healing for _____

(Mention anyone else that you feel healing is really important for today. Gently squeeze the hand of the person to your left to indicate that it's their turn. Let everyone have a turn at saying this part before continuing with the script.)
- We send our healing thoughts to Mother Earth and to the plant and animal kingdom. Thank you.
- Release your hands but keep your eyes closed so that you remain relaxed and peaceful as we go in to our meditation. *(Brief pause before moving on to the Meditation script.)*

THEORY: NATIVE AMERICAN WISDOM & TOTEM ANIMALS
The following 'theory' section should be read aloud to the group. You may want to get others to join in and take it in turns to read.

Many people find that they have a Native American Guide when they begin their spiritual and psychic journey. Why is this? Some people have even been heard to say, 'I hope I don't have a Native American Guide, it's such a cliché'. However, the reason that they appear as Guides fairly frequently is firstly that they are so recognisable, as well as powerful, evocative and symbolic to us. Also, might we be a little disappointed if our first guide was a guy who appeared in jeans and jumper and looked like the local butcher? Secondly, the essence of their culture has a lot of wisdom to offer, especially to those of us who now live so detached from nature.

Like all indigenous cultures around the globe, the native people of North America were finely attuned with nature. They understood their connection with, and interdependence on the earth, and constructed their stories around all natural phenomenon. They lived in tune with nature's cycles and honoured all plant and animal life. Aspects of the body, mind and spirit were not divided but fully integrated and there was a deep reverence for, and understanding of, the spirit realms.

All native cultures, wherever their place on the earth, have all used symbols from nature to invoke certain energies or powers. Signs and symbols in nature also hold great importance, especially to the shamans who act like the tribe's priests. This symbolism is used strongly in the two subjects we are going to touch on in this lesson: 'Totem Animals' and the 'Medicine Wheel'.

ABOUT TOTEM ANIMALS:

In Ted Andrews book 'Animal Speak', he states that "a totem is any natural object, being or animal to whose phenomenon and energy we feel closely associated with during our life".

In the same way that we have different types of Spirit Guides, we can have a number of different totem animals. They help and guide us in different ways. We may have one or more dominant totem animal that stays with us throughout our entire life. They can help us to understand ourself and our life path. We may have different animals that appear during certain phases or projects within our life to give us guidance or a particular type of energy.

We may observe animal symbolism around us, which can act as pointers or messages in the same way that other symbols do. They can appear in our dreams, during readings or in everyday life in actual animal form, or as pictures, symbols or they may even be brought up continually in conversation.

When we feel drawn to a particular animal, are repeatedly visited by them in some way, or see them in our everyday life, it's interesting to look more closely at their attributes and associations, their symbolism and their essence, or their power. This is described in shamanic cultures as their 'medicine'. It can help us to learn more about ourselves, our path and things that are going on around us at any given time.

We can also call upon animal medicine and integrate it into our own energy when it's needed. This can help to give us certain qualities that we feel we might otherwise lack, such as a boost of confidence, understanding of the bigger picture, more sensitivity to others, focus, attention to detail and much more.

THE MEDICINE WHEEL:

'Medicine' in shamanic cultures is really an essence or energy that helps your connection with all aspects of yourself, with those around you, humanity and nature. It's about healing on many different levels; mind, body and spirit and learning how to live in harmony with the Universe.

The 'Medicine Wheel' is created as a physical symbol of all of the things in the Universe, including those in and around ourselves. It can be used so that we can learn, usually through meditation, how to align ourselves with them and bring them into our reality.

The 'Medicine Wheel' can be very complex and involved, however, for our purposes we will work with a simplified version. When set up outside, a circle of stones is created with larger stones or rocks used to represent the four compass points. These should be placed correctly aligned with the directions. Indoors it could be created with crystal points or large stones that you have collected, perhaps from a beach.

To use this tool, you can take time to meditate whilst sitting at each point in turn, focussing your attention on the energy of the direction. Perhaps you have a question or problem that relates to those things it assists with. So, in meditation you could state that you wish to approach the Totem Animal relating to that direction and ask for it's wisdom and guidance.

PRACTICAL WORK

Read out each exercise, one at a time to the group so that you are all clear as to what you are doing, then allocate a time to complete the exercise.

As with Spirit Guides, the best way of communicating with your Totem Animals is through meditation, so we have altered the order of things for this lesson.

EXERCISE 1: Meditation
- Ensure that you're sitting comfortably with your hands on your knees, palms facing upwards.
- Close your eyes.
- Take a deep inhalation, and breathe out slowly. Continue to breathe slowly and deeply.
- During this meditation you will always be safe and protected, you will feel relaxed and comfortable. If, however, there is anything that does make you feel uneasy, or you wish to come back out of the meditation, you can do so at any time by counting backwards from 3 to 1 and taking a deep breath in and out. You can then bring your awareness back to the physical body, particularly your feet and open your eyes.
- For now though, continue to breathe slowly and deeply, your body feels relaxed and your mind is clear.
- As you breathe images may begin to form in your mind's eye. Don't try to manipulate or analyse them, simply observe them. If you do not automatically see these images, simply imagine or sense them.
- Ahead of you lies a staircase or series of ten steps. Move towards them. At the bottom you can see a doorway. We're going to slowly go down these steps towards the door feeling safe and confident at all times. So moving down the steps on my count:
- 10, 9, 8, with each step feeling lighter and lighter.
- 7, 6, 5, feeling calm and peaceful,
- 4, 3, relaxed and light
- 2 and 1, you find yourself standing in front of the door. Reaching out you open the door and as you do so, a wonderful, warm light shines through from the other side, bathing your whole being in its rays.
- As you stand in this light for a few moments, your physical body is warmed through and your energy body is nourished and energised. This gives you a sense of comfort and completeness and offers further protection on your journey. *(Pause for a short while)*
- Today's journey is designed to help you to connect with the energy of the Totem Animal that is required in your life at this moment in time.
- The rays of light subside and you can now see through the doorway to your sanctuary on the other side.
- You step through the doorway now, closing the door behind you and make your way to the exit that leads to your garden or outside space. Or your sanctuary could be outside.
- Ahead of you you see a pathway stretching far ahead into the distance. It may even fork off in different directions stretching to the right and to the left. Choose the direction that you feel most comfortable with, and begin walking along the pathway.
- As you walk along the pathway be aware of the sights and sounds around you. Above you is a beautiful bright blue sky and you are surrounded by the warmth of the sun's rays. As you walk along the pathway you find that around you the landscape is changing and it now resembles a land from far away with mountains surrounding you, glistening lakes and vibrant, colourful plants and trees wherever you look. Breathe in the pure clean air.
- Continue walking until you find a comfortable place to stop and sit down. You may find yourself by the edge of a river, or under the shade of trees. You are safe and protected wherever you choose to sit. As you sit down, be aware of all of the sounds around you. You become aware of an animal's call. It's a sound that seems very familiar to you and not frightening in any way. As you listen, the animal draws closer to you, becoming clearer to you. You're happy to see the animal, you know that it won't harm you, but comes to befriend you.
- Allow the animal to come to your side. As you look into its eyes you immediately recognise it and your souls connect. You know that this special animal comes to bring you wisdom and knowledge. If you wish to you can reach out and touch your totem animal. Perhaps you will speak together, as you have the ability to transcend all normal restrictions and can communicate both verbally and telepathically. I will leave you together for a while and I will return for you shortly. *(pause for 3-4 minutes)*
- It will soon be time to leave your totem animal. Bid it farewell, and then watch it as it moves away

from you. Remember that you will take away with you all that you've learnt from your magnificent totem animal, and that everything you have seen, felt or experienced will remain with you, at least in your subconscious, on your return.
- Begin walking back along the pathway that brought you to your special meeting place, again observing all the wonderful sights and sounds surrounding you. Look at the majestic mountains, the glistening lakes, the lush vegetation, breathe in the wonderfully pure air. With each step you take along the pathway, you feel more and more energised, yet still calm and relaxed.
- Continue walking until you see the door that leads back into your sanctuary. Walk through this familiar place to the doorway leading to your stairwell.
- Open the door that leads to the stairwell. Step through closing the door behind you.
- Know that your sanctuary is your own space that you can return to at any time for relaxation, guidance and healing.
- And keeping that sense of calm and wellbeing, it is time to head back up the stairs.
- So moving back up the stairs on my count, 1, 2, 3, breathing slowly and deeply,
- 4, 5, 6, your body is starting to feel heavier
- 7, 8, bringing your awareness back to your physical body,
- 9 and 10, on that top step now and when you're ready, step off the top step.
- **Bringing your awareness completely back to your physical body and this room, your contact with the chair, your feet with the floor. Slowly begin to move your fingers and toes, and in your own time, opening your eyes, fully awake and aware and in the physical world.**
- *(Watch for them starting to wriggle fingers and toes and keep an eye on anyone who doesn't do this. If a member of the group appears not to want to come back to the room simply repeat the last paragraph, in bold, but raising your voice so that it said slightly louder and firmer. Repeat a third time if necessary moving over to the person and at the end just saying their name and asking that they come back now in to the room, placing your hand gently on their shoulder.)*
- Following the meditation take time to make some notes of your journey and if working with friends, spend a few minutes sharing your thoughts and experiences.
- Take some time to look up the animal symbolism and see what their main qualities are and what that might help you with in your life right now. Make a note of this too for your records.

EXERCISE 2: The Medicine Wheel
- Set up a simple medicine wheel by placing four large stones or crystal points at the North, East, South and West of the room. Or if you're lucky with the weather and have the space, why not do this outside?'
- Photocopy and cut out each 'Compass Point Card. The relevant 'Compass Point Card' should be placed under each stone, or pinned to the wall as a guide.
- Each of you should take some time to walk around the circle, pausing at each of the four points for as long as you wish. Focus your intention on receiving the most appropriate energy that you need at this moment in time.
- When you feel it's appropriate, choose the direction that you are most drawn to.
- Take a look at the 'Compass Point Card' and see if the correspondences relate to what is going on in your life at them moment, or to any particular question or concern that you may have.
- Sit at this direction and allow yourself time to tune into its energy. Meditate on it for a while. What images, thoughts or feelings come to you? How does it make you feel?
- If possible, allow each person to choose which point they wish to sit at and then all sit quietly and meditate on it's energy for a few moments.
- Discuss this with each other and see if you or someone else can shed any light on the reason for your choice.
- Makes notes on your experiences and thoughts ensuring that you date them.

EXERCISE 3: Totem Animal Card Readings
- If you have time to do some further work and you have or can borrow a pack of Animal Cards, you could have a go at one of the following:
- Choose a card from the pack with the focused intention that you would like either to know your life path or an animal totem for the following week, month or year.
- Once you have chosen a card, you can take a look in any books you have or at our 'Animal Symbolism' guide as to the significance of the animal but also have a discussion with anyone you are working with and take into account your beliefs and opinions of the animal and what it could teach you. Again make a record of your cards, messages and thoughts.
- Additionally you can pair up and read your cards for each other, in the same way as you did with card reading exercises in Lesson 8.
- If you don't have any animal cards to use, have a group discussion and see if anyone has an animal that repeatedly shows up for them at this time. Read about and discuss its relevance in the same way.

CLOSING & GROUNDING

Once you have completed the exercises and had some discussion time, everyone should sit comfortably and complete the following meditation to close and ground their energy. Read aloud the following: (or use the audio CD.)

- Sit in a comfortable position and close your eyes.
- Bring your attention to your breathing and focus on this for a few breaths. *(Pause)*
- Take your awareness to the invisible energy field surrounding you and visualise it drawing in close around your physical body. *(Pause)*
- Take your awareness to the area just above your crown and see a sphere of light sitting here.
- Imagine that sphere of light shrinking in size until it's tiny, then sinking down through the crown of your head.
- See it slowly descending down past the brow. *(Pause)*
- Into the throat. *(Pause)*
- Then following the line of the spine, down, through your body, towards your heart area. (Pause)
- Down to your solar plexus. *(Pause)*
- Through the abdominal area. *(Pause)*
- To the base of your spine. *(Pause)*
- Now visualise the sphere of energy either leaving through the base of your spine, or dividing in two and sinking down through your legs and leaving through the soles of your feet.
- Feel this energy leaving you and connecting with the earth.
- Have a sense of downward movement, deep in to the earth. *(Pause)*
- Become more aware of your feet and your physical body.
- Let us take a moment to thank our Spirit Guides, Angels and loved ones in Spirit for their presence, protection and wisdom whilst we've been working. Knowing that they will always be on hand should we need to call on them. *(Pause)*
- **Now bring your awareness back to your physical body, the chair you are sitting on and your contact with the floor.**
- **Begin to bring some movement back in to your fingers and toes.**
- **In your own time opening your eyes, fully awake and aware and in the physical world.**

(Watch for them starting to wriggle fingers and toes and keep an eye on anyone who doesn't do this. If a member of the group appears not to want to come back to the room simply repeat the last three points, in bold, but raising your voice so that it said slightly louder and firmer. Repeat a third time if necessary moving over to the person and at the end just saying their name and asking that they come back into the room now, placing a hand gently on their shoulder.)

Check to ensure that everyone feels grounded before you finish the session. If not, get them to walk around for a little while. Stamping your feet or jumping up and down helps to bring you back to the physical world. If these don't do the trick, you can ground your energy very readily by eating a small amount of food such as a biscuit.

AND ANOTHER THING:
- A great book for animal symbolism is 'Animal Speak' by Ted Andrews
- Try working some more with the medicine wheel. You could work with it once a week for four weeks, experiencing each of the four main directions in turn. Have an open mind and allow its energy to show you your way. You may fall asleep and dream, you may receive images, sensations or colours in your mind's eye. Or you may simply feel at peace and more centred. Make a note of your experiences.
- There are lots of books on Native American Wisdom. Anything by Kenneth Meadows is worth taking a look at and you can often borrow them from your local library. Helen attended one of his weekend retreats and found it to be a profound experience, he was a very interesting and inspiring man.
- Pay more attention to repeated visits by specific animals or an unexpected visit by an unusual animal. They can also be sent in the form of pictures or images and objects such as ornaments and jewellery. Keep a record of it, and its symbolism in your journal. How does it relate to you now? Is it a message or confirmation that you're on the correct path?

Next Time...
The next lesson will be covering WORKING WITH SPIRIT.
You will need to arrange for the following tools to be brought along:
- A selection of different coloured fabrics, shawls, scarves or pashminas. If you don't have any, repeat the ribbons exercise on page 32 (lesson 2).

LESSON TWELVE
WORKING WITH SPIRIT

PREPARATION
Well in advance of your meeting ensure that you have all of the tools that you require for this lesson. If not, find out if another group member has access to what you need.

Regular tools:
- Healing book
- Pens and pencils
- Paper
- Candles & matches if desired
- Box of tissues

Tools for this lesson:
- A selection of different coloured fabrics, shawls, scarves or pashminas. If you don't have any, repeat the ribbons exercise on page 32 (lesson 2).

On the day of the meeting ensure that the room is prepared:
Are there enough seats for everyone and enough room for the work you are about to undertake?
Open the windows or burn some incense to freshen the air.
Gather the required tools together. Call and remind anyone who has promised to bring something.
Set out some water and glasses.
Prepare some relaxing background music.

At the beginning of the meeting:
As people arrive ask them to add the names of anyone they know who needs some healing to the Healing Book. Remember that you don't need to put their full names and private information, first names, initials or nicknames will suffice. Whoever you intend to send the healing to, it will reach.

Once everyone has arrived and is comfortable then you can start.
Work your way through the script and exercises for this lesson as detailed on the following pages.

OPENING & PROTECTION
Read the following script out loud to the group. It's a time of meditation so keep your voice calm and relaxed, reading in a fairly slow and controlled manner. Instructions are in brackets and italics. (Alternatively use the audio CD.)

- Let us take a moment to close our eyes and calm our minds.
- Concentrate on your breathing, allowing the breath to become deeper and slower.
  (Pause to allow everyone to take a couple of breaths in and out)
- Let us all mentally ask our Spirit Guides and Angels to draw close and create a circle around our own.
- We let it be known that we are happy to work with Spirit and that we only work in love and light. We ask that anyone from the spirit world who wishes to contact us only does so in love and light and with the highest intentions.
- We ask for your protection, guidance and wisdom as we blend our world with yours. *(Pause)*

- Let us blend and harmonise our energies as we sit together in circle.
- Let us send out a note of harmony to the person on our left. Visualise this as a pale pink mist coming from your heart area and moving towards the heart of the person sitting on your left. *(Pause)*
- As you continue to do this, become aware of receiving the same loving energy from the right.
- As we send and receive this energy, be aware of any changes in the atmosphere within the circle. *(Pause)*
- Have a sense of oneness with the group. *(Pause)*
- Now bring your attention back to yourself and the centre of your being, the lower abdominal area.
- Focus on your breathing; become aware of the rise and fall of your abdomen. As you inhale it will gently rise and as you exhale it will fall. *(Pause to allow everyone to take a few breaths in and out)*
- Have a sense of warmth here and in your mind's eye allow a symbol or shape to form. Imagine that this symbol or shape is sitting at and represents your centre. It may be a simple glow of light, a flame or a flower.
- With each in-breath visualise your symbol becoming larger, stronger or more open whichever is appropriate.
- With each out-breath, imagine that you are exhaling any negativity left from your day, or worries that you may have. *(Pause to allow everyone to take a few breaths in and out)*
- Now take your awareness to the soles of your feet, feeling their contact with the floor. Visualise lines of energy extending out from your feet and down into the ground. In your mind's eye, see these lines of energy as roots extending deep into the earth.
- Earth energy also travels back up through these roots revitalising and nourishing you.
- See this energy entering through the soles of your feet and travelling up through your legs to the base of your spine.
- At the base of the spine imagine that the energy becomes a sphere of deep red mist or light, as you visualise it, it becomes more vibrant in colour. *(Pause)*
- From this point a beam of energy leaves the red sphere and travels up towards the sacral area, just below the belly button. Here it forms a sphere of vibrant orange mist or light. As you focus on it, it becomes stronger in colour. *(Pause)*
- Gradually a beam of energy leaves the orange sphere and travels up towards the solar plexus, where it forms a sphere of clear yellow. With each breath, this yellow becomes stronger and brighter. *(Pause)*
- Once more a beam of energy leaves this sphere and continues its journey up to the heart area. Here a sphere of mist or light begins to form, which you may see as either green or pink. Focus on this area for a few breaths allowing the energy to grow stronger and clearer and to expand. *(Pause)*
- Gradually a beam of energy leaves the heart area and moves upwards to the throat. Here it forms a sphere of clear blue. Once more, as you focus on this area, allow the colour to expand and increase in strength. *(Pause)*
- Now, visualise a strand of energy leaving the throat area and linking with the third eye area, just between and slightly above the eyes. Here energy will begin to form as before. You may see this energy as either a rich indigo or violet, whichever you prefer. Concentrate on this energy and visualise it increasing in strength. *(Pause)*
- Again, a beam of light extends upwards from this area moving to the crown. As it does so, become aware of another beam of energy coming down from above to meet the first. As they meet at the crown a sphere of pure energy begins to form. You may see this energy as either violet or pure white light. This connects you with the higher realms of Spirit.
- As you hold this vision for a few breaths the light grows and strengthens. And as it does so, the beautiful pure light begins to overflow down and around you, surrounding you in its wonderful energy. It fills your aura, cleansing, balancing and strengthening it. You feel safe and comfortable. You feel relaxed and light. *(Longer pause before moving on to the Healing script below.)*

HEALING
- Slowly open your eyes and join hands with those sitting to either side of you. This increases the flow of healing energy.
- We know that our Guides, Angels and loved ones in Spirit have come forward and that they surround us with their healing energies. We ask them to help us as we send out our healing today. *(Pause)*
- Visualise a pool of brilliant white light forming and growing in the middle of our circle. *(Pause)*
- This is a pool of healing energy from which we can all draw when we need to. Know that this universal healing energy will find its way to all of those for whom we request healing.
- We ask for healing for each of us here, for our minds, bodies and spirit.

(If there are absent members: We ask for healing for the members of our group who cannot be with us today.)
- We ask for healing for all of those on our Absent Healing List. Take a moment to visualise them standing the healing pool.
- I would also like to ask for special healing for _____

(Mention anyone else that you feel healing is really important for today. Gently squeeze the hand of the person to your left to indicate that it's their turn. Let everyone have a turn at saying this part before continuing with the script.)
- We send our healing thoughts to Mother Earth and to the plant and animal kingdom. Thank you.
- Release your hands but keep your eyes closed so that you remain relaxed and peaceful as we go in to our meditation. *(Brief pause before moving on to the Meditation script.)*

MEDITATION
- Ensure that you're sitting comfortably with your hands on your knees, palms facing upwards.
- Close your eyes.
- Take a deep inhalation, and breathe out slowly. Continue to breathe slowly and deeply.
- During this meditation you will always be safe and protected, you will feel relaxed and comfortable. If, however, there is anything that does make you feel uneasy, or you wish to come back out of the meditation, you can do so at any time by counting backwards from 3 to 1 and taking a deep breath in and out. You can then bring your awareness back to the physical body, particularly your feet and open your eyes.
- For now though, continue to breathe slowly and deeply, your body feels relaxed and your mind is clear.
- As you breathe images may begin to form in your mind's eye. Don't try to manipulate or analyse them, simply observe them. If you do not automatically see these images, simply imagine or sense them.
- Ahead of you lies a staircase or series of ten steps. Move towards them. At the bottom you can see a doorway. We're going to slowly go down these steps towards the door feeling safe and confident at all times. So moving down the steps on my count:
- 10, 9, 8, with each step feeling lighter and lighter.
- 7, 6, 5, feeling calm and peaceful,
- 4, 3, relaxed and light
- 2 and 1, you find yourself standing in front of the door. Reaching out you open the door and as you do so, a wonderful, warm light shines through from the other side, bathing your whole being in its rays.
- As you stand in this light for a few moments, your physical body is warmed through and your energy body is nourished and energised. This gives you a sense of comfort and completeness and offers further protection on your journey. *(Pause for a short while)*
- Today's journey is designed to help you to strengthen your links to the spirit world and communicate with that dimension if you wish to.
- The rays of light subside and you can now see through the doorway to the other side. As you look ahead you see the shapes of a forest forming. Step through the doorway and make your way towards it. It is a magical, enchanted forest. The trees seem to be alive, their leaves gently rippling in the cool

summer's breeze. You feel safe and happy as you enter the forest. You notice a carpet of beautiful woodland flowers surrounding you, the colours of the flowers more vibrant than you have ever seen before. You may be aware of the sounds of woodland animals, insects and birds.

- As you walk through the forest you are amazed by the beauty and the serenity of this magical place. All of your senses seem heightened, and you feel connected to everything around you.
- As you continue walking you find a beautiful lake in the middle of the forest. The emerald green water sparkles in the sunlight that streams through the treetops. By the side of the water is a safe, comfortable, inviting place to sit down. As you sit down, touch or drink some of the refreshing water if you want to.
- Allow yourself to relax further, letting thoughts drift out of your mind. With each moment that passes you feel more and more connected to your surroundings. As the connection grows, so does the intensity of everything around you. The sounds become clearer. The scents become more fragrant. The sights become more defined. Anything you touch feels softer and more pure than ever before. Take a few moments to enjoy this connection. *(Pause for a few moments).*
- As you continue to relax, you become aware of someone else walking towards you. Perhaps you can see them. Perhaps you can hear them. Perhaps you can sense them, or smell them, or perhaps it is a combination of any of these things. You feel safe and secure and know that the person who comes to you only does so in love.
- Take a few moments to acknowledge how you know they are there. Which senses connect you to them? Be aware that that connection is amplified so that it becomes very easy for you to communicate with them.
- Now you're aware of them sitting by your side. You may know them, or recognise them on some level, or perhaps it's the first time you've met. Remember that they come to you with love. You're able to communicate with them easily. I am going to leave you for a time now to speak to them and spend time with them. I will return for you shortly. *(Pause for 5 minutes)*
- It's now time to begin your journey back, so take a few moments to bid your companion goodbye. Know that the connection between you can never be broken and that they will come back to talk to you whenever you ask them to. Feel secure in the knowledge that you'll take back with you everything that you've shared during your time together.
- Feeling energised and happy, you rise from the place by the lake, and begin walking back through the forest. You are still aware of the deep connection you have with everything around you and that your senses are still heightened, and will remain so on your return.
- Continue walking until you see the door through which you came.
- Open the door that leads to the stairwell. Step through closing the door behind you.
- Know that your sanctuary is your own space that you can return to at any time for relaxation, guidance and healing.
- And keeping that sense of calm and wellbeing, it is time to head back up the stairs. So moving back up the stairs on my count,
- 1, 2, 3, breathing slowly and deeply,
- 4, 5, 6, your body is starting to feel heavier
- 7, 8, bringing your awareness back to your physical body,
- 9 and 10, on that top step now and when you're ready, step off the top step.
- **Bringing your awareness completely back to your physical body and this room, your contact with the chair, your feet with the floor. Slowly begin to move your fingers and toes, and in your own time, opening your eyes, fully awake and aware and in the physical world.**

(Watch for them starting to wriggle fingers and toes and keep an eye on anyone who doesn't do this. If a member of the group appears not to want to come back to the room simply repeat the last paragraph, in bold, but raising your voice so that it said slightly louder and firmer. Repeat a third time if necessary moving over to the person and at the end just saying their name and asking that they come back now in to the room, placing your hand gently on their shoulder.)

Spend a few minutes sharing experiences of the meditation. Remember that it's okay if someone fell asleep, could see nothing or did their own thing. If you're keeping a personal journal, you may wish to take some time to record you experience. Don't forget to date the entry.

THEORY: WORKING WITH SPIRIT
The following 'theory' section should be read aloud to the group. You may want to get others to join in and take it in turns to read.

Many people see, feel or hear spirit naturally, particularly as a child. As they get older their skills often diminish. This can happen for a number of reasons: fear of being told that they're imagining things or making it up, because it's not actively developed or simply because they get side-tracked by other things in life. For some it is only when a spirit is particularly strong or emotionally linked to them that they're aware of their presence. One example would be following the death of a loved one.

When developing the skills associated with linking with Spirit it's important to differentiate between everyday activities and psychic work. It's quite distracting to be interrupted at work by Great Uncle Albert who wants to pass on a message to your mum!

It's also important to be able to connect or communicate with our Spirit Guide(s) and to understand how to 'open', 'close', and 'protect' our energies. That's why this subject is at the end of the workbook – do not be tempted to jump ahead to this one without doing the groundwork!

Using all of our senses is usually second nature in the physical world. It's known that if someone loses one of their senses the others become stronger to help counter the affects of the loss. For example, a blind person will often have a more finely tuned sense of hearing and smell. They're just as important to us when working in a psychic or spiritual way. Any or all of our senses can be called into play. By developing these senses both on a physical and the more subtle level we can use them to far greater effect in meditations and when receiving messages for ourselves and others. Understanding our senses and how they relate to psychic work is important.

- Sight - Clairvoyance is translated as 'to see clearly'. Some people are able to physically see spirit, symbols and messages that need to be passed on to others. Some people can also see the auras or subtle energy systems of others, either naturally or through practise.
- Hearing - Clairaudience is translated as 'to hear clearly'. Some people are able to hear messages from spirits and Guides which can be passed on to others.
- Scent - This sense is amazing as its centre in the brain is so close to our memory centre that smells and memories are often powerfully linked. Some people will be aware of scents that are manifested by a spirit to announce their presence. Scent can also have a physiological effect on us causing us to relax or to become more active.
- Taste - Some people find that this sense is activated when working with Spirit.
- Feel: - This can have two different associations when working with Spirit. Feeling in a physical sense: some people are physically touched by spirit to let them know that they're present; and in a more subtle or 'knowing' way, others sense or 'feel' their presence. 'Clairsentience' is translated as 'to sense clearly' and most mediums work, in all or part, in this way. It's often a case of 'knowing' something that is being passed on as a message from Spirit.

Mediums and psychics use a combination of methods to communicate with Spirit. By now you will probably have an idea of which method you find the easiest. It's best to concentrate on developing in this area first and then to diversify. You'll also find that as you develop in one way, the other methods will become easier and you will start to advance naturally with a combination.

So, to recap, the main forms of spirit communication are:
- clairaudiency - hearing
- clairvoyancy - seeing
- clairsentiency - sensing

Clairsentience seems to be the most common method of working. It's possibly the easiest skill to develop yet the hardest to explain. Initially you will find that you simply 'feel', know or think things. You may see with your mind's eye (a mix of clairsentience and clairvoyance) or hear with your mind's ear (a mix of clairsentience and clairaudience). Eventually, with practise, you may find that you start to see physically or hear audibly, however, if you don't that's fine. The important element is the ability to extract the message and pass it on to those in the physical world. Part of that skill is to learn the signs and symbols given to you, usually by your Guide and, again this comes with experience.

It's useful to think of our Guides as the 'mediums' of the other side, in the same way that we are the 'mediums' of the physical world. We both stand in the middle, at the edge of our own world, with one foot in the other. It's at this point that we can communicate with each other on behalf of those who find it difficult to do so, and pass on the messages accordingly.

HELEN & DIANE'S TIPS:
- Symbolism is used a lot in this kind of work and it's important to find out how symbols work for you and what they mean to you, rather than going with a book's definition. For example, if Helen sees an image of a pumpkin, it could be that she needs to give the message that she sees a pumpkin, or it can also mean that Halloween or October / November is a significant time for the person she is speaking to, or it can represent the end of a cycle.
- For some mediums, whereabouts they feel a spirit around them or the enquirer can often be relevant. Basically, spirit will often stand on a particular side of you, or the person you're reading for, to represent either the maternal or paternal link. This helps you to place them within the context of the family tree. This takes experience and a degree of trial and error to translate, which is why working with a group, is so important. You can practise until you know which way round it works for you, i.e. Does spirit on the left represent them being linked to the mother's side or the father's side?
- As with all of these subjects it's important to find the way that things work for you, and this can take time. Mediums spend many years honing their skills. You may find that you work best in a very quiet meditative state. Others find that they need to engage in conversation with the enquirer in order to raise the energy and link into their vibration, and therefore any spirit who may be around them.
- Remember protection. Always ask for protection before you start any practical work. Say the following or something similar, 'We are happy to communicate and work with Spirit, but we only work in love and in light and we ask that anyone who steps forward to communicate with us also only does so in love and in light'. Use this if you are practising at home, along with the opening visualisation, surrounding yourself in white light and asking your Guides to step forward and offer their protection and guidance.
- Please note, we are not summoning spirit. We are 'tuning in' in order that we can communicate with those who wish to make themselves known to someone in the physical world. Imagine you're at your front door, you're opening it to see if there is anyone there with a message. You aren't standing there yelling for someone, anyone, to come and talk to you. Really, anyone could turn up. Equally, when you're done, don't forget to close the door for security reasons - that's, of course, closing and grounding.

LESSON TWELVE - WORKING WITH SPIRIT

PRACTICAL WORK
Read out each exercise, one at a time to the group so that you are all clear as to what you are doing, then allocate a time to complete the exercise.

IMPORTANT NOTE: If anyone feels uncomfortable or fearful at anytime, stop. Have a break, have a laugh to raise the energy vibrations back up to a more comfortable level, and then try again if you wish.

EXERCISE 1: Warm Up
- Work in Pairs.
- One person from each pair should sit quietly with their eyes closed (the reader).
- Gather together the selection of coloured fabrics, scarves or pashminas and place them in a pile or on a table behind the chairs, so that the readers cannot see them.
- The partners should all choose a piece of coloured fabric from the collection and drape it gently over their reader's shoulders.
- The reader should attempt to sense the energy from the fabric. What feelings or images pop into your head? Tell your partner who can make notes for you.
- If the reader is struggling, their partner can prompt them with questions like, 'What was the first thought that came to mind?', 'How are you feeling?', 'Do you have any sensations at any of the chakras points?', 'If so, which ones?'
- The reader may wish to guess at the colour of the fabric, it's worth a go!
- It's also worth keeping your notes so that you can look at what that colour did for you. It all adds to the toolbox that you're building up to enhance your abilities and skills.
- Swap over so that everyone gets a turn.
- If you don't have the fabric or shawls required, repeat the ribbon exercise from page 32 (lesson 2).

EXERCISE 2: Work Out
- One method of connecting with spirit presences is to expand your own energy field so that it encompasses the energy of the spirit in the room. This is actually very simple and similar to previous exercises that we've done. Read the instructions before you start so that everyone knows what they are doing.
- Sit quietly in a circle and close your eyes.
- Take your awareness to the outside of your physical body and then to the energetic body surrounding you.
- As you inhale imagine your auric energy expanding in all directions around you.
- Spend a few minutes doing this so that your aura is as large as you can imagine it to be, but stays within the confines of the room you're in.
- Mentally scan your aura checking for any energies that have crossed over from others in the room.
- Do you feel anything different or unusual? What pops in to your head? Are you aware of any feelings as though someone is standing near to you or to someone else in the room?
- If you feel any changes in energy or receive any images, words, names, or a message, speak out. Simply say something like, 'I am getting a cold breeze just behind me', or ' I have the word 'primrose' in my head'. Someone may be getting the same experience or know what you're referring to. Discuss what you're sensing and experiencing, keeping your voice calm so as not to disrupt the energy.
- Keep a dated record of your experiences and any feedback or confirmation that you get.

EXERCISE 3: Tune In
- The meditation in this lesson, along with previous exercises, should have given you a clue as to the way you will connect best with Spirit: clairaudiently, clairvoyantly or clairsentiently. You can use that information now to help you to link in.
- Sitting quietly in your chair and cast your mind back to your meditation. What sense(s) helped you to connect to your spirit visitor?
- Now concentrate on this sense. If you heard them, it may help to close your eyes to increase the focus on your hearing. Likewise if you saw them, it may help to cover your ears, so that the focus increases on your sight. If you sensed them, again close your eyes and take note of anything that you begin to feel (this may be physical or a 'sense).
- Ask your companion from your meditation to step forward and communicate with you again. Remember the heightened connection that you still have after your meditation. Be aware of anything that you sense, see or hear even if it's very subtle. Ask them to make a definite communication, and see if you get anything different.
- After a few minutes bring your awareness back to the room and discuss your experiences with the each other.
- Keep a dated record of this exercise.

EXERCISE 4: Get Connected
- This can be attempted in pairs or in groups. It's good to try both. You may find that you're more successful when working as a group as there's increased energy when you all connect and join together.
- Hold hands with you partner or in a circle, if working with a larger group. This is crucial to enable the energy to build up.
- Expand your auric energy as you did in exercise 2.
- If you wish to, you can ask (either individually in your head, or with one person speaking on behalf of the group) for anyone from the world of spirit to communicate with you if they so desire.
- Be aware of anything you see, sense, feel or hear.
- After a couple of minutes, take some time to swap anything that you have experienced with your group/partner. Remember to 'give what you get'. Something that you experience may mean nothing to you, but may be a very important and meaningful message for someone else you're working with.
- Discuss all of your experiences and findings from these exercises with the group.
- Keep a dated record of your experiences.

CLOSING & GROUNDING
Once you have completed the exercises and had some discussion time, everyone should sit comfortably and complete the following meditation to close and ground their energy. Read aloud the following: (or use the audio CD.)

- Sit in a comfortable position and close your eyes.
- Bring your attention to your breathing and focus on this for a few breaths. *(Pause)*
- Take your awareness to the invisible energy field surrounding you and visualise it drawing in close around your physical body. *(Pause)*
- Take your awareness to the area just above your crown and see a sphere of light sitting here.
- Imagine that sphere of light shrinking in size until it's tiny, then sinking down through the crown of your head.
- See it slowly descending down past the brow. *(Pause)*
- Into the throat. *(Pause)*
- Then following the line of the spine, down, through your body, towards your heart area. (Pause)
- Down to your solar plexus. *(Pause)*
- Through the abdominal area. *(Pause)*
- To the base of your spine. *(Pause)*
- Now visualise the sphere of energy either leaving through the base of your spine, or dividing in two and sinking down through your legs and leaving through the soles of your feet.
- Feel this energy leaving you and connecting with the earth.
- Have a sense of downward movement, deep in to the earth. *(Pause)*
- Become more aware of your feet and your physical body.
- Let us take a moment to thank our Spirit Guides, Angels and loved ones in Spirit for their presence, protection and wisdom whilst we've been working. Knowing that they will always be on hand should we need to call on them. *(Pause)*
- **Now bring your awareness back to your physical body, the chair you are sitting on and your contact with the floor.**
- **Begin to bring some movement back in to your fingers and toes.**
- **In your own time opening your eyes, fully awake and aware and in the physical world.**

(Watch for them starting to wriggle fingers and toes and keep an eye on anyone who doesn't do this. If a member of the group appears not to want to come back to the room simply repeat the last three points, in bold, but raising your voice so that it said slightly louder and firmer. Repeat a third time if necessary moving over to the person and at the end just saying their name and asking that they come back into the room now, placing a hand gently on their shoulder.)

Check to ensure that everyone feels grounded before you finish the session. If not, get them to walk around for a little while. Stamping your feet or jumping up and down helps to bring you back to the physical world. If these don't do the trick, you can ground your energy very readily by eating a small amount of food such as a biscuit.

AND ANOTHER THING:
- Go along to an open evening of clairvoyance at a local spiritualist church or similar. Find out more about how others work and see what you pick up while you are there.
- Discuss as a group how far you have come, your achievements and what you would like to do next.
- You may also find it interesting to read autobiographies of mediums, which can give you useful and interesting insights into how they communicate with Spirit.

WHERE NEXT?

THE NEXT STEP
This course of lessons can be repeated as often as you wish. You will always benefit from the information, exercises and meditations. You may feel confident enough to investigate other subjects further yourselves, or alternatively, our 'Advanced Workbook' will allow you to continue your development within the same structure as this one.

FINAL THOUGHTS
We hope that you've enjoyed your journey through the variety of subjects that this workbook has covered and that you've found a subject that you enjoy, are good at and want to pursue further. There's never an end point in this game, we're always learning and experiencing new things. Just as we start to feel comfortable with what we are doing, 'they' up the ante and we find ourselves off on a new path all over again. However, each time we do, we're endowed with more skills and knowledge than the last time. We may even appear to be revisiting old ground, but there's always something new to experience, or we look at it with new eyes and a greater awareness and understanding.

Your challenge is to step up and meet life head on, step into the flow and feel the power of life as it takes you on the journey that you were destined to travel. Enjoy the experiences and the people that you meet, bask in the light, use what you learn to help pull you through the rough patches, knowing that *you* are an integral part of life and that *it* is an integral part of you. Neither can exist without the other. And eventually we will all find our way home again.

With Bright Blessings on your path, wishing you love and light always,
Helen & Diane

APPENDICES

HANDOUT 1
INTRODUCTION

WHAT WE WILL COVER
Meditation, Auras & Chakras, Colour, Spirit Guides, Healing – hands-on & absent, Psychometry, Crystals, Dowsing, Tarot / Card Reading, ESP / Telepathy, Divination, Scrying, Totem Animals, Working or linking with Spirit / Mediumship.

RULES
1) Do not mix your spirits!
In other words, no alcohol, or other mind-altering substances for that matter! Being under the influence whilst working in circle affects your ability and judgement. It also lowers your energy vibration and your defences (in much the same way as it lowers inhibitions). This can leave you and the rest of the group open to less positive energies or influences. This is non-negotiable.

2) Confidentiality.
Anything of a personal nature must not be spoken of outside of the group. This will allow everyone to work with trust and develops a safe and supportive environment. This does not mean that spirit are going to divulge your innermost secrets to everyone, they don't work like that, but discussions can arise which can bring up sensitive issues and everyone needs to know that they can be open and honest with each other.

3) Stay Positive!
This is extremely important. Positive energy is essential when working in a circle. If you feel negative, depressed or simply under the weather, tell the group or take a break and get an early night instead. You will be told how to bring yourself out of a meditation should you feel the need, and if ever feel worried or uncomfortable in the group you must mention it. It would be wise to change the subject for a few minutes or to lighten the mood a little.

GUIDELINES
- Please be Prompt - If you know that you are going to be late let a group member know in advance so that they can wait for you.
- Keep it Regular - whilst it is understandable that things do crop up which can't be helped, it is preferable for group members to attend regularly to maintain group harmony.
- Food - it is not advisable to eat a large meal *just* before circle, equally a rumbling tummy during a meditation can be off-putting. Many people prefer to avoid eating meat before circle as they believe that it lowers their vibratory rate making it more difficult to work with the higher, faster spiritual energies.
- Health - if you're unwell it isn't advisable to work in circle as your energy levels will be low, but let the group know and they'll send you healing energy to help you feel better! If a person suffers from depression, anxiety or a similar mental health issue, especially if they are on medication for any of these conditions, we would strongly suggest that they avoid working with Spirit. They're more vulnerable to energy dips and should concentrate on getting well before developing in this way. However, learning about and taking part in healing groups would be beneficial.
- Personal Hygiene - a lot of books and teachings say that one should ritually prepare for spiritual work by bathing and dressing in particular clothing before starting work. This is not always possible, or necessary, however, cleanliness is always appreciated! Heavy perfumes can interfere with psychic work so should be avoided.

© 2009 www.spreadingthemagic.com

HANDOUT 1 CONTINUED
INTRODUCTION

- Sharing - please do! Don't be worried about saying something silly, all contributions are welcome.
- Comparing - please don't! Everyone develops at different rates and finds certain things easier than others. Don't feel that you have to be the same as someone else or that you're not good enough, learn from and encourage each other.
- Working Space - it is ideal to use the same room each week. Before the meeting the room should be prepared. If possible, open the windows and air the room earlier in the day. Ensure that the room is warm and comfortable and that there is enough seating for everyone in the circle. You may want to burn some incense or place some fresh flowers in the room.

You may like to keep your own journal. One of the best ways to do this is to use an A4 ring binder. Then you can section it off as you wish with dividers, and use it to keep the handouts that are included on this course. You can add interesting magazine and newspaper articles that you find and record your own meditations and discoveries. Also, if you forget to take your folder to a lesson or on a course, you can make notes and slot them in at a later date. You will soon build up an amazing reference guide for yourself as well as having documenting your journey and development.

APPENDICES

HANDOUT 2
CHAKRAS DIAGRAM

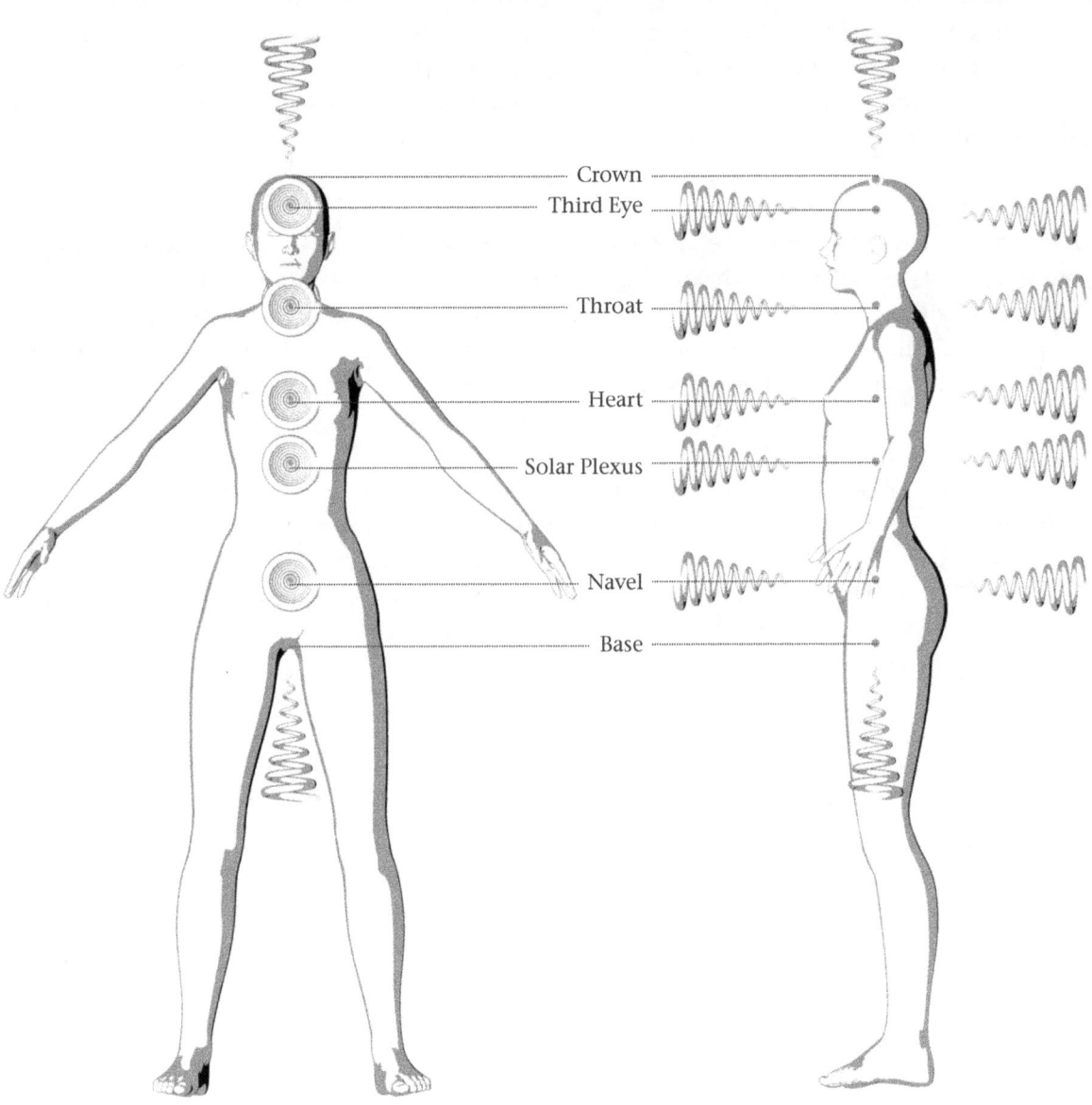

© 2009 www.spreadingthemagic.com

HANDOUT 3
BASIC CHAKRAS INFORMATION

BASE CHAKRA - RED

Located at the perineum, this chakra opens downwards. It connects us to the physical world, keeps us grounded, and is said to be the seat of the collective unconscious. If this chakra is too open we may be overly concerned with materials things, possibly self-indulgent. If this chakra is too closed we may be run down physically, have a tendency to worry too much, or feel 'away with the fairies'. If this is the case, grounding work is important to keep our feet on the ground.

SACRAL CHAKRA - ORANGE

Located two fingers below the navel. It's related to our primordial emotions, security, sexuality, empowerment and creativity. If this chakra is too open we may crave a more meaningful relationship, not realising that the most important one is with ourself. We may need to be more embracing of the miracles of nature. If this chakra is too closed we may withdraw from the attention or sensual signals from others, life may seem a bit boring and we may need to learn to express our feelings.

SOLAR PLEXUS CHAKRA - YELLOW

Located at the diaphragm, this chakra is our power centre, it connects us to the astral body and it helps us to perceive the vibrations of others. If this chakra is too open we may be too open to the energies of others and need to learn to protect ourselves. The automatic reaction of folding our arms over this area if feeling uncomfortable helps prevent us from picking up negativity from others or our surroundings. If this chakra is too closed, we may be insensitive to others' energy or to our surroundings. We may need to learn to extend our awareness and be more observant.

HEART CHAKRA - GREEN (SOMETIMES PINK)

Said to be the seat of unconditional love. This chakra is related to healing, empathy and sympathy. It connects us to the spiritual aspect of ourselves and others. If this chakra is too open it's possibly as a result of constantly putting others before ourselves. A closed down heart chakra is often found in those who don't like themselves or find it difficult to trust or love others. We may need to learn to be kinder to and forgive ourselves.

THROAT CHAKRA - BLUE

This chakra relates to expression, communication (including listening) and inspiration. It connects us with the mental auric body. An overly open throat chakra is common among public speakers or those who feel driven to communicate continually for whatever reason. A closed down throat chakra is found if we're unable to communicate our feelings with others, or if we do not listen to others, or notice signs around us.

HANDOUT 3 CONTINUED
BASIC CHAKRAS INFORMATION

THIRD EYE OR BROW CHAKRA – INDIGO OR VIOLET
Located slightly above and between the eyes. This chakra relates to psychic perception and intuition and is said to connect us to all levels of creation. If this chakra is too open we may be too focused on intellect and reason, try to rationalise everything and influence the thoughts of others. If this chakra is too closed we may only accept what we can actually see, be forgetful or lose our head in a crisis. In either case we may benefit from developing our intuitive and psychic side.

CROWN CHAKRA - VIOLET OR WHITE
Located on the crown of the head, this chakra opens upwards. It's related to universal knowledge and connects us to the spiritual plane. The crown chakra becomes more open with spiritual advancement. It can't be too open. The crown is always connecting us to Spirit, however, if it appears small or narrow, you may wish to actively pursue a more spiritual path.

THE SPIRITUAL & PSYCHIC WORKBOOK – A COURSE COMPANION

HANDOUT 4
BODY / CHAKRAS OUTLINE

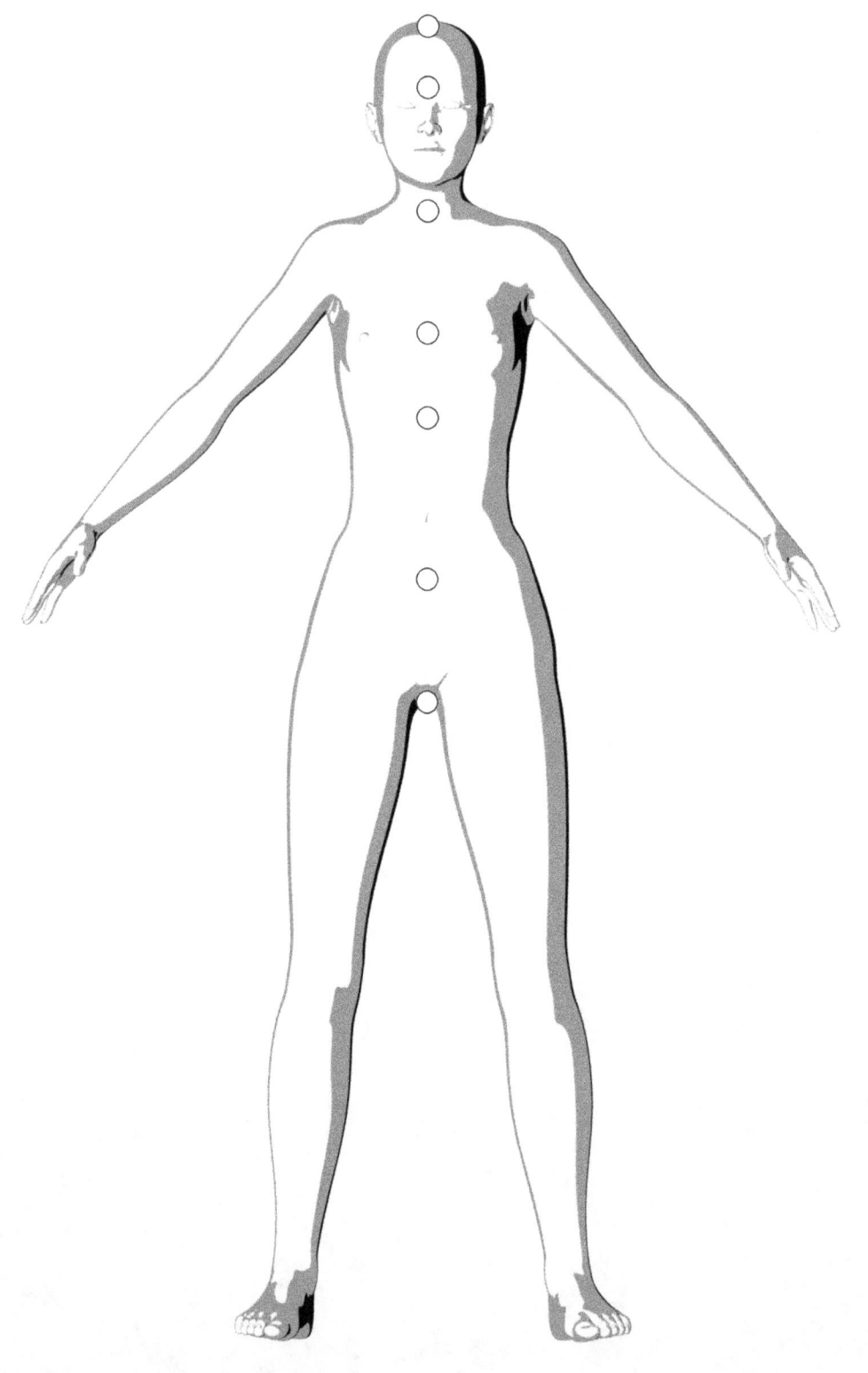

© 2009 www.spreadingthemagic.com

APPENDICES

HANDOUT 5
BASIC COLOUR INFORMATION

RED
If you surround yourself with, love the colour or have lots of **RED** in your aura you are: Passionate, active, courageous and strong with lots of vitality.
Caution: Too much exposure can cause anger, impulsiveness and hunger.
Use RED to: Add some get up and go to your life.

ORANGE
If you surround yourself with, love the colour or have lots of **ORANGE** in your aura you are: Joyful and happy, an optimistic, independent and social person.
Caution: Too much can cause restlessness.
Use ORANGE to: Cheer yourself and give you confidence.

YELLOW
If you surround yourself with, love the colour or have lots of **YELLOW** in your aura you are: Intellectual, creative and artistic. An open and articulate person.
Caution: Over exposure can cause over-thinking, over-analysis or being too open to the affect that others can have on you.
Use YELLOW to: awaken clairsentient abilities and to bring happiness into your life.

GREEN
If you surround yourself with, love the colour or have lots of **GREEN** in your aura you are: Affectionate, loyal and trustworthy. You are full of sympathy and compassion and strive for health and harmony.
Caution: Too much green can mean that you let others walk all over you or have a tendency to seek peace at any price.
Use GREEN to: Promote calm, relaxation, healing and balance.

PINK
If you surround yourself with, love the colour or have lots of **PINK** in your aura you are: Charming and delicate, a peacemaker, full of love and compassion,
Caution: Over exposure can lead to indecisiveness, immaturity and lack of focus.
Use PINK to: Attract love, protection and security and to learn to appreciate the finer things in life.

BLUE
If you surround yourself with, love the colour or have lots of **BLUE** in your aura you are: Good at communication, listening skills and self-expression. You are serious and cautious. Blue is linked with clairaudience.
Caution: Too much can mean someone who is over cautious, a worrier or is oversensitive.
Use BLUE to: attract tranquillity, and to learn to communicate your concerns.

© 2009 www.spreadingthemagic.com

HANDOUT 5 CONTINUED
BASIC COLOUR INFORMATION

PURPLE
If you surround yourself with, love the colour or have lots of **PURPLE** in your aura you are: Strong, sensitive, spiritual and intuitive. It is linked with clairvoyance and E.S.P. You're a visionary and are passionate about your beliefs.
Caution: Over exposure can cause you to be overbearing, feel misunderstood and become aloof.
Use PURPLE to: Develop your spiritual and psychic side.

WHITE
If you surround yourself with, love the colour or have lots of **WHITE** in your aura you are: A very spiritual person, an idealist and an innovator. You may seem shy but you do voice your opinions. You are seeking and are aware of the process of enlightenment.
Caution: Over exposure may cause you to begin to think of yourself as more important than others.
Use WHITE to: Help simplify your life, seek the truth and awaken greater creativity.

BLACK
If you surround yourself with, love the colour or have lots of **BLACK** in your aura you are: Seeking knowledge, intense, introspective and have hidden depths.
Caution: You may be trying to hide in the shadows or be suppressing your desires.
Use BLACK to: Look within.

APPENDICES

HANDOUT 6
PENDULUM COLOUR CHART A

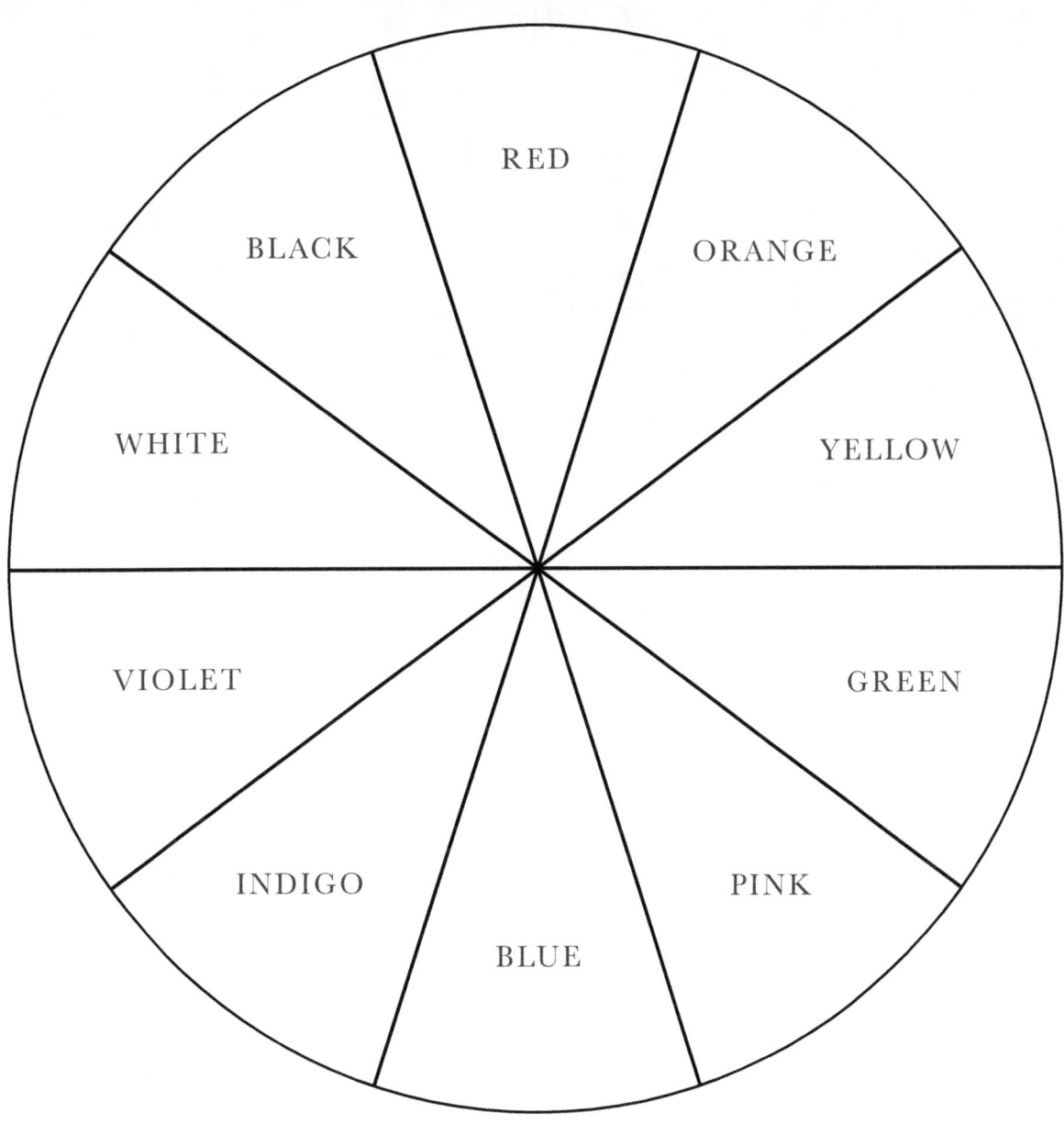

© 2009 www.spreadingthemagic.com

THE SPIRITUAL & PSYCHIC WORKBOOK – A COURSE COMPANION

HANDOUT 6
PENDULUM COLOUR CHART B

RED
ORANGE
YELLOW
GREEN
PINK
BLUE
INDIGO
VIOLET
WHITE
BLACK

© 2009 www.spreadingthemagic.com

APPENDICES

HANDOUT 7
CONNECTING WITH YOUR SPIRIT GUIDE

- Sit down in a quiet place, if at all possible where you are unlikely to be disturbed.
- Some people like to light a candle or have appropriate crystals with them.
- You may work with your eyes open or closed - whatever helps you to focus more easily.
- Have paper and a pen close at hand for any pictures or messages that you may get.
- Before you start remember to ask your Guides, Angels and loved ones in Spirit to draw close and surround you with their love and protection. State that you only work in love and light.
- Ask your guide to come forward to communicate with you.
- Relax, and start to listen to your thoughts.
- Say 'Hello' to your guide. In your mind, you should sense or hear a greeting in reply.
- Say 'I would like to know your name'. If you have trouble understanding the name, listen hard, then come as close as you can to what you sense or hear. Spirit will accept whatever name you give them! Some names are long and make have to be shortened - or a letter of the alphabet substituted.
- Say 'May I call you _____'. You will sense whether or not that name seems right to use – change it if you want to. Once you get a name that you sense is right for you and your Spirit Guide, proceed on to other questions.
- Ask any other questions you would like to. Wait for an answer. It should be immediate.
- When you've finished, say 'Goodbye and god bless' and thank your Guide for working with you.
- Close yourself down – visualise the tree roots growing from your feet, through the floor and into the centre of the earth.

© 2009 www.spreadingthemagic.com

HANDOUT 8
BASIC CRYSTAL INFORMATION

WHAT DO CRYSTALS SAY ABOUT YOU?

Amethyst: You are highly spiritual or seeking your spiritual path. This stone enhances intuition and psychic abilities and encourages personal development. Is that what you do, or what you need to do?

Black tourmaline Highly protective & grounding, this stone helps to banish fear. Is that what you need right now? Or are you looking for a solution to a problem? It could be close to hand. Listen to your intuitive flashes.

Citrine: The stone of abundance, wealth and success. Are you looking for more focus? Are you starting a new relationship, job or project? You are being guided and success is indicated.

Clear quartz: Do you feel that you need to move things along? Are you looking for a higher purpose? This stone indicates enhanced psychic abilities, good health and more energy. Engage with your inner strength to facilitate success and achievements.

Green aventurine: Future growth and expansion. This stone indicates that a balance of male and female energies is required or is happening. Do you need to make a decision right now? This stone can help you to make the right one.

Haematite: Do you need more calm and reason in your life, especially in a relationship? Calm your mind, become clear about what you want and turn the negatives into positives.

Jasper: Pay attention to earthly matters. Have you been letting things slide recently or ignoring something that needs to be dealt with?

Pyrite: A strong masculine stone. Do you need to be more confident and take control? All may not be as it seems, read between the lines and keep an eye out for deception. Do you need the energy to put ideas into practise? Make a practical action plan to get to where you want to be.

Rose quartz: A warm, healing, loving stone. Indicates healing capabilities. Can also indicate that you need to open your heart more, especially to yourself. Forgiveness and release of old emotions may be required so that you can move on with love.

Sodalite: Do you need to learn to communicate better? This includes listening! Or are you developing your Clairaudient skills? Maybe you should. Is your mind muddled and in need of clarity?

Tigers eye: Are you lacking in confidence? Need to be more independent? This stone indicates a change for the better. It attracts beauty, abundance and practical wisdom, do you? If not, maybe you will now, or is that what you transmit to others?

© 2009 www.spreadingthemagic.com

HANDOUT 9
3-CARD SPREAD

| PAST | PRESENT | FUTURE |

Or
events that have
led to…

Or
…the current situation
or question…

Or
…the possible outcome,
future assistance or choices.

© 2009 www.spreadingthemagic.com

THE SPIRITUAL & PSYCHIC WORKBOOK – A COURSE COMPANION

HANDOUT 10
ZENER CARD SYMBOLS

© 2009 www.spreadingthemagic.com

APPENDICES

HANDOUT 11
ESP RESULTS RECORD PAGE

Name of Sender: ....

Name of Receiver: ....

Date: ....

Score: ....

	Symbol sent	Symbol received
1		
2		
3		
4		
5		
6		
7		
8		
9		
10		
11		
12		
13		
14		
15		
16		
17		
18		
19		
20		
21		
22		
23		
24		
25		

© 2009 www.spreadingthemagic.com

THE SPIRITUAL & PSYCHIC WORKBOOK - A COURSE COMPANION

HANDOUT 12
PSYCHIC SYMBOLS

It would be impossible to list all of the images that you might encounter, but here are a few interpretations that may help you unravel the symbolism. Whilst it's good to have a guide, it's your interpretation that counts. Ask yourself, does it ring true for you? Also the symbol itself may be of significance for the person you are reading for so you may want to tell them exactly what you see.

Angel: A desire to become more spiritual or to rise above more earthly and everyday matters. Represents a peaceful outcome.
Birds: Generally birds are a symbol of freedom. Although you can get more specific such as a dove for peace, a raven for deceit, and a peacock warning of pride.
Butterflies: Spiritual transformation.
Bridge: Crossing to new things. Take note of what lies on either side.
Cat: Associated with female qualities, your intuition or your psychic self. Also with good fortune ahead.
Church: The sacred will be of importance to you.
Door: A new phase or opportunity in your life.
Faces: Does the face represent an emotion or state of mind? Does it remind you of someone you know? They may be a key figure for you in the future.
Fish: Fish are a universal symbol of life and fertility.
Hat: A change of job or life role.
Horse: A horse can represent untamed emotions or even sexual ecstasy.
Horseshoes: A symbol of good luck to come.
Judge: Are you required to make a decision? Is something playing on your conscience? Or it could represent a future conflict with authority.
Keys: A problem solved or a new opportunity.
Knife: You may need or wish to cut some ties. Someone may mean you harm.
Ladder: Progress or promotion.
Moon: The moon has always been linked with the feminine, fertility, intuition and emotion. It may represent personal growth or travel overseas.
Mountains: A quest and possibly obstacles along the way.
Owl: Wisdom.
Path: The direction you are currently taking in life. Are there any other symbols around? Is there a crossroads or a decision to be made? Is it smooth, or littered with obstacles?
Pig: Are you being stubborn, selfish or brutish? Or is that someone around you?
Policeman: Are you feeling guilty? Do you have an issue with authority?
Queen: Representative of a motherly figure, or that side of your own nature. Listen to your intuition.
Rose: A symbol of love.
Storm: Are you feeling overwhelmed by some inner conflict? A possibility of trouble ahead.
Spider: Weaving or creating your life. Or a possible fear of being trapped, especially if it's in its web.
Train: Could represent the direction of your life. Don't miss an opportunity.
Tree: Strong yet flexible. Is that your message? Can also represent being in touch with the earth, and old wisdom.

© 2009 www.spreadingthemagic.com

APPENDICES

HANDOUT 13
ANIMAL SYMBOLISM

Alligator: Aggression, survival and adaptability.
Ant: Patience, team and community spirited, a worker.
Armadillo: Relating to personal boundaries.
Bat: Rebirth, guardian of the night, helps you to know what and who to avoid.
Bear: Introspection, heal the sick, power, inner strength, courage and wisdom.
Black panther: Embracing the unknown.
Buffalo: Prayer and abundance, a provider and protector, sacredness, life-builder.
Butterfly: Transformation, metamorphosis, carefree.
Crane: Solitude, independence, intelligence, learning and keeping secrets; reaching deeper mysteries and truths.
Crow: Keeper of the Sacred "Law" of the universe, gateway to the supernatural; thief, trickery, a bringer of knowledge; prophecy, shape-shifting, divination.
Deer: Gentleness, kindness, love.
Dolphin: Knowing the unknowable, kindness, play, in touch with the inner child.
Dog: Loyalty, tracking skills, even through conflicting or confusing situations, companionship, keen hearing, tenacity, protection; finding out the truth. If you see a dog in meditation, you will be guarded from approaching danger.
Dove or Pigeon: Communicating with friends and loved ones in spirit; spiritual messenger between worlds; peace, gentleness, love.
Dragonfly: Flighty, carefree, removing restrictions, Change. Illusion, life is not what it seems to be.
Eagle: Connection to the heavens, freedom and power, courage, wisdom and keen sight.
Falcon: Sees hidden spiritual truths and the overall pattern of life. Rising above the material looking for spiritual direction. Linked to astral travel, healing, releasing the soul of a dying person.
Fox: Quick, decisiveness, camouflage, protector of the family unit, intelligence and cunning, a provider.
Hawk: Messenger from the heavens, an observer, clear-sightedness; helps in recalling past lives, messages from spirit, omens and dreams.
Hedgehog: Child-like innocence and humility, protection.
Heron: Ability to watch patiently for results, methodical processes, gaining dignity and self-confidence, self-reflection.
Horse: Physical and unearthly power, stamina, mobility, strength and sexuality.
Hummingbird: Joy, happiness and love.
Lion: Learn to relax and let go of stress, strengthen family ties, strength and courage.
Lizard: Dreaming, conservation, agility.
Magpie: Omens and prophecies, the mysteries of life and death, divination of any kind.
Mouse: Scrutiny, there is more to learn.
Otter: A very female medicine, joy for others, laughter, curiousity, mischievous.
Owl: Clairvoyance, astral projection, magic, wisdom, truth and secrets. Unmasking those who would deceive you, patience, guide to and from underworld, shape-shifting, omens and moon magic.
Parrot: Imitation, mockery, think carefully before you speak; don't repeat gossip.

© 2009 www.spreadingthemagic.com

HANDOUT 13 CONTINUED
ANIMAL SYMBOLISM

Peacock: Dignity, self-confidence, warning of pride coming before a fall. The peacock "eye" may represent seeing into the past or future.
Rabbit: Fear, alertness, nurturing.
Raven: Magic, helps with divination, a change in consciousness, messages from Spirit, something unforeseen but special is about to occur.
Snake: Transmutation, sexuality, shrewdness.
Spider: Weaving, creation, creating your own life.
Squirrel: Gathering, harvesting.
Swan: Grace, balance, innocence; spiritual evolution, divination, transitions.
Tiger: Power, energy, action.
Turtle: Mother Earth, goddess energy, creative source.
Wolf: A Teacher. Confidence, strength, honour our emotions, trust our intuition.

APPENDICES

HANDOUT 14
COMPASS POINT CARDS

The directions & their native american correspondences are listed here and can be copied and cut out to provide compass point reference cards when working with the medicine wheel.

NORTH
The energy of the north helps to clarify our thoughts and works with the mind. It is associated with renewal, purity, clarity, the mind and intelligence.
Totem Animal: Buffalo
Colour: White
Time of Year: Spring

EAST
The energy of the east provides flashes of inspiration and understanding. It is associated with light, both of the inner more esoteric and the outer, physical sort. It is also linked with dispersing darkness, ignorance and negativity, awakening, newness of life, far sightedness, revealing the truth and spirituality.
Totem Animal: Eagle
Colour: Yellow
Time of Year: Summer

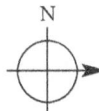

SOUTH
The energy of the south activates and strengthens the intuitive side of ourselves. It is associated with personal growth, discovery, teaching inner knowing, emotions, closeness and vitality.
Totem Animal: Mouse
Colour: Red
Time of Year: Autumn

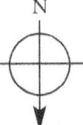

WEST
The energy of the west assists the physical body and enables it to work efficiently and harmoniously. It is associated with transformation, introspection, endurance and stability.
Totem Animal: Grizzly bear
Colour: Black
Time of Year: Winter

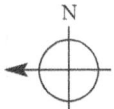

© 2009 www.spreadingthemagic.com

GLOSSARY OF TERMS

Please bear in mind that these are our explanations of these terms, you may find other slightly different definitions.

3rd Eye: Refers to the brow chakra is located between and slightly above our eyes. This chakra is used for and related to psychic work and remote viewing.

Advanced / Highly Evolved Beings: Beings from the 'Spirit' or 'higher' realms with insight and knowledge of Universal wisdom and laws. They transcend the physical dimension as well as time and space.

Angel Cards: Used in a similar way to Tarot but with pictures depicting different types of Angels. Other cards are also available depicting mythical creatures and other scenarios.

Circle: A group of like-minded individuals who meet regularly in order to develop their spiritual beliefs and psychic or mediumistic abilities.

Divination: The practise of seeking information by paranormal means. Examples are the use of cards, tea leaves and runes.

Electro-Magnetic Field: The residual energy produced by and emanating from any atomic structure. Probably caused by the constant movement of its minute parts.

Empathic: Usually referring to those who understand and share the feelings of others. Within the context of psychic work, this term refers to the ability to 'feel' and, possibly, experience the emotions of others. Very often people aren't aware that they're empathic but find it very easy to build rapport and understand others. They also feel a strong urge, almost a responsibility to help people.

Guided Visualisation: A form of meditation whereby a very descriptive narrative of a journey or experience assists those taking part in imagining or seeing it in their mind's eye.

'Into The Light': The term used when the spirit of a deceased person moves on into the Spirit Realm. So called as many people who have near death experiences describe moving towards a bright light.

Medium: A person who is able to communicate with those in the Spirit Realm.

Paranormal: According to the Oxford English Dictionary, this means, "supposedly beyond the scope of normal scientific understanding".

Pendulum: A suspended weight able to swing freely. In our context usually a crystal, glass or metal object. Used as a tool for divination.

Psychic: The ability to know or have access to information through 'paranormal' means.

Psychometry: The art of providing a psychic or mediumistic reading by tuning into the energy vibrations of an object worn or carried close to the enquirer, or their deceased loved one.

Reiki: A Japanese term meaning 'Universal Life Force Energy' which has come to describe a particular 'school' or method of healing.

Rescue: A spiritual and psychic practise for helping earthbound spirits to move on into the Spirit Realm. A 'rescue circle' is a group of experienced mediums and healers who specialise in performing rescue work.

Runes: A set of small tablets or stones each marked with a single letter of an ancient Germanic alphabet, used for divination purposes.

GLOSSARY OF TERMS

Scrying: The practise of using a reflective surface or object, such as water, a crystal ball or dark mirror, to 'see' symbols, acquire information or to connect and communicate with Spirit.

Spirit: The essence, perhaps soul, of a person that continues to exist beyond physical death of the body. Often referring to the non-physical world beyond our own where we come from before and pass on to after our life. In this book we indicate the latter meaning by use of a capital 'S'.

Spiritual: Being aware of the interconnection of everything living and of the essence or spirit that makes each of us alive and unique. Having an understanding that there's more to life than physical matter and that a part of us continues to exist after physical death.

Spiritualist Church: Meeting places, not normally actual churches, for Spiritualist Meetings which usually include demonstrations of mediumship, healing evenings and often workshops and development groups. Services are run along similar lines to regular churches with prayers and hymns but a Spiritualist Church is looking to provide proof of the existence of spirit after physical death.

Supernatural: According to the Oxford English Dictionary, "attributed to some force beyond scientific understanding of the laws of nature".

Sympathetic vibration: The phenomenon by which a system is encouraged to vibrate at its natural frequency by energy from a nearby system vibrating at that same frequency.

Telepathic / Telepathy: The ability to send or receive thoughts, words or images to or from another individual by means other than the 'known' senses.

© 2009 www.spreadingthemagic.com

RESOURCES

WHERE TO GO FOR HELP:
It's difficult for us to recommend a particular place or person without knowing them personally and having had some experience of their work. However, these are some points of contact for you that will start you off if you're in need of help. Do a bit of research in your local area, ask for recommendations and trust your intuition. (UK only)

To help you find a local Spiritualist Church visit the Spiritualist National Union's website: www.snu.org

For courses, seminars and demonstrations take a look at The Arthur Findlay College in Stansted, Essex. Their website is www.arthurfindlaycollege.org

The Pagan Federation for honest and reliable information about the many types of pagan faith. www.paganfederation.org

If you have any further questions or would like to leave comments, reviews or discuss any of the subjects covered in this book visit www.helpithinkimightbepsychic.com

Other Websites associated with and personally recommended by the authors:

www.spreadingthemagic.com
An on-line resource for personal, spiritual and psychic development. Books & products, courses, workshops and other events. Plus, sign up for a free e-newsletter.

www.stmpublishing.co.uk
For all books & products by Spreading The Magic.

www.protectedbyangels.co.uk
Find out more about healing, and put someone in the online healing book if you feel they could benefit from help by our angels.

www.spreadingthewealth.co.uk
Exploring wealth vs. spirituality, the metaphysics of abundance and ways to save & make money

www.petalsinthewind.co.uk
Information on courses and workshops on psychic development held in Hertfordshire.

www.lighting-the-way.co.uk
A website offering enlightenment and upliftment to those wishing to explore their spiritual side.

RECOMMENDED READS

Books that we've found useful relating to subjects from this workbook

Psychic Protection by Judy Hall
The Crystal Bible by Judy Hall
How To See and Read The Aura by Ted Andrews
How To Meet and Work With Spirit Guides by Ted Andrews
How To Do Psychic Readings Through Touch by Ted Andrews
Animal Wisdom by Ted Andrews
The Telepathy Kit by Tara Ward
Medicine Cards - book and cards by Sams and Carson
Where Eagles Fly by Kenneth Meadows
Voices in My Ear (and other books) by Doris Stokes
Spirited By Tony Stockwell
Angel Cards & Fairy Cards by Doreen Virtue

Also see our own list of Other Books & Products

ABOUT 'SPREADING THE MAGIC'

Started in 2005 by Helen Leathers, 'Spreading The Magic' began life as an online resource for personal, spiritual and psychic development. Courses and workshops and a small range of products were available. Helen was also writing and had a number of projects on the go at once. But she knew it was extremely difficult to get an agent or publisher in the literary world. So she decided to create what she wanted and pull the two concepts together turning 'Spreading The Magic' into a publisher for her and Diane's specialist books on the spiritual side of life.

'Spreading The Magic' is a vehicle with which we seek to help others find and develop their own spirituality and integrate it into their daily life.

Our core values are open-mindedness and acceptance.

We want everyone to find their own path and know their own truth. To find the magic in themselves and to see it in others.

The 'magic' is our connection with life, our oneness with the universe and everything within it. Through our courses, workshops, articles, books, products, websites and events we aim
To encourage, inform and inspire
To simplify and demystify the unknown
To open hearts and minds
To promote non-judgement, acceptance and understanding
To transform and enlighten
To leave a positive impact
To teach others to create their reality
To raise consciousness, personally, socially and globally
To remember
To Be
To spread the magic

Become part of the change at www.spreadingthemagic.com

OTHER PRODUCTS FROM HELEN & DIANE

These can be ordered using the form on page 155 or online at www.stmpublishing.co.uk

Help! I Think I Might Be Psychic
101 Frequently Asked Questions About Spiritual, Psychic & Spooky Stuff
Answered by Helen Leathers & Diane Campkin

This book is for everyone who has ever asked. "What's it all about?", "Is there life after death?", "What's it like to see a ghost?" and other virtually unanswerable questions.

Do you have fascination with or passing interest in the paranormal?

Do you have a more pressing concern and don't know where to turn for the answers?

Do you suspect you have a talent, a path, a dream or desire that you are not fulfilling and you really wish there was more to life?

Whether you have had supernatural experiences or not, this book will give you the basics, and a whole lot more. This is our take on the often confusing and occasionally egotistical world of the paranormal. A reference point that's open and honest and that looks to blow away some of the cobwebs surrounding the more esoteric side of life and death, as we see it. This book is for everyone. Do you want to know more...?

RRP £7.95

Bright Blessings

Spiritual Thoughts, Inspirational Quotes and Philosophical Observations on Life.
By Helen Leathers

Ever wonder about the bigger picture and the spiritual side of life?

Do you need inspiration? Are you happy?

Do you truly know who you are and where you're heading?

This is a collection of articles, observations and quotes which aim to make you stop and think. Whether you need inspiration, a quiet moment, a focus for meditation, spiritual or philosophical advice or support, or maybe something different to do this weekend, this is the book to have within easy reach.

RRP £5.95

The Spiritual & Psychic Development Workbook

A Beginners Guide
by Helen Leathers & Diane Campkin

An introduction to the theory and practical basics of spiritual and psychic development. From meditation to dowsing, card readings to working with the chakras, understanding crystals to connecting with your Spirit guides.

Do you want to increase your intuition, work with healing energy, learn how to meditate or develop your own clairvoyant ability?

This book will facilitate an opening up to and development of your own natural spirituality and psychic skills. Essential basics, simple to understand theory and practical exercises make this a beginners guide for everyone. And there's not too many long words either.

This is the book we've been looking for for years.

RRP £9.95

WATCH OUT FOR...

MEDITATIONS AVAILABLE ON CD
Read by Helen Leathers & Diane Campkin. Available to order from www.stmpublishing.co.uk

CD1 Essential Beginners
Suitable for use on its own or to accompany either our 'Beginners Guide' or 'Course Companion'. Includes 'opening & protection', and 'closing & grounding' visualisations, 'Creating Your Sanctuary' PLUS a bonus track.

CD2 Individual meditations from our Course Companion Workbook Lessons 2 - 7.
Includes 'Meeting Your Spirit Guide', 'Extending Your Senses' & 'Connect with the Energy of the Earth'

CD3 Individual meditations from our Course Companion Workbook Lessons 8 - 12.
Includes 'Awaken Your Psychic Senses' & 'Connect With Your Totem Animal'.

THE POWER IN YOUR HANDS
An Experiential Guide to Energy Work
by Helen Leathers
This book is an introduction to the basics of energy work for aspiring healers, lightworkers and anyone seeking personal, spiritual or psychic development.
It's a hands-on, practical approach to understanding the theory behind the subtle energy systems of the universe. Learn how to connect to, channel and consciously focus universal energy and integrate energy work into all aspects of your life.
Whether you feel that you personally need more energy or you would like to work with energy for healing, spiritual or psychic work, this is a great place to start.
this book provides the building blocks of theoretical and practical understanding which will allow you to make your journey at your own pace, develop your own ideas and skills and enjoy your path to enlightenment and empowerment.
Want a more fulfilling life? The power is in your hands.

THE SPIRITUAL & PSYCHIC DEVELOPMENT - AN ADVANCED WORKBOOK
Following on from 'A Beginners Guide' our advanced workbook will offer further information on developing your growing skills as well as new, more advanced subjects to try.
An Advanced Workbook Course Companion will also be available for groups and workshop leaders.

Register for updates and offers on these or find out more at:
www.thepsychicworkbook.com
or www.stmpublishing.co.uk

www.ingramcontent.com/pod-product-compliance
Lightning Source LLC
Chambersburg PA
CBHW080910230426
43666CB00013B/2662